Available titles in the series:

Mapping the Magazine: Comparative Studies in Magazine Journalism
Edited by Tim Holmes

The Future of Newspapers
Edited by Bob Franklin

Language and Journalism
Edited by John Richardson

The Future of Journalism
Edited by Bob Franklin

Exploration in Global Media Ethics
Edited by Muhammad Ayish and Shakuntala Rao

Foreign Correspondence
Edited by John Maxwell Hamilton and Regina G. Lawrence

How Journalism Uses History
Edited by Martin Conboy

Lifestyle Journalism
Edited by Folker Hanusch

Environmental Journalism
Edited by Henrik Bødker and Irene Neverla

Online Reporting of Elections
Edited by Einar Thorsen

The Future of Journalism: Developments and Debates
Edited by Bob Franklin

Cross-continental Views on Journalistic Skills
Edited by Leen d'Haenens, Michaël Opgenhaffen and Maarten Corten

Cross-continental Views on Journalistic Skills

This book considers the role journalism education plays in coping with a changing media landscape. It looks at how journalists can empower themselves in an effort to excel in an evolving environment and considers whether it suffices for them to master 'pre-millennial' basic skills or whether brand new competencies need to be incorporated.

Few dramatic qualifications are spared when discussing the changes that have shaken the news world during the noughties. Digitization has both empowered and tried professional journalists through multimedia news production, media convergence and not least a maturing commercial internet. Moreover, digitization has also influenced, and been influenced by, other societal changes such as global financial tensions, evolving multicultural societies, and emerging democracies in search for a suitable journalistic paradigm. Indeed, the rather technological evolutions emphasized time and again, cannot be detached from a cultural setting. This is why an investigation in required competencies benefits from an explicit socio-cultural and cross-continental perspective. As this book tackles a varied set of 'news ecosystems', it is our hope to offer a nuanced view on what indeed seems to be a global fluidity in journalism practice.

Explicit emphasis is put on the role of journalism education as facilitator for, and even innovator in, required journalistic competencies. Time will tell whether or not 'news ecosystems' will again stabilize. This volume makes a number of recommendations towards journalism training and discusses a number of case studies across several continents, illustrating how goals are attuned to a changed news environment. As this book links academic paradigms to concrete journalism practice and education, its reading is recommended both for practitioners and educators.

This book was originally published as a special issue of *Journalism Practice*.

Leen d'Haenens is Professor in Communication Science at the Institute for Media Studies, KU Leuven, Belgium, where she teaches Media and Diversity, Western Media Policy, and Analysis of Media Texts. Her current research interests include cross-national news frame analyses of the Euro-crisis, Islam and Muslims, the study of commercial and public service broadcasters' diversity potential, and the study of power relations and alliances with regard to issues relevant to the multicultural society in mainstream and online media (ethnic discussion forums, blogs) in North-Western Europe.

Michaël Opgenhaffen is an Assistant Professor at the Institute for Media Studies, KU Leuven, Belgium, and at the University of Leiden, The Netherlands. He teaches New Media and Society and Social Media Research in the master's programs in journalism. His research focuses on the use of social media in journalism practice, on the changing nature of journalism, and on the possible mismatches between journalism education and journalism practice.

Maarten Corten was a Teaching Assistant in Communication Science at the Institute for Media Studies, KU Leuven, Belgium, from 2010 till 2012. Together with Michaël Opgenhaffen and Leen d'Haenens he is the co-author of *Nieuwsvaardig, een crossmediale competentiematrix voor journalisten* (Leuven, 2011).

Journalism Studies: Theory and Practice

Series editor: Bob Franklin, Cardiff School of Journalism, Media and Cultural Studies, Cardiff University, UK

The journal *Journalism Studies* was established at the turn of the new millennium by Bob Franklin. It was launched in the context of a burgeoning interest in the scholarly study of journalism and an expansive global community of journalism scholars and researchers. The ambition was to provide a forum for the critical discussion and study of journalism as a subject of intellectual inquiry but also an arena of professional practice. Previously, the study of journalism in the UK and much of Europe was a fairly marginal branch of the larger disciplines of media, communication and cultural studies; only a handful of Universities offered degree programmes in the subject. *Journalism Studies* has flourished and succeeded in providing the intended public space for discussion of research on key issues within the field, to the point where in 2007 a sister journal, *Journalism Practice,* was launched to enable an enhanced focus on practice-based issues, as well as foregrounding studies of journalism education, training and professional concerns. Both journals are among the leading ranked journals within the field and publish six issues annually, in electronic and print formats. More recently, 2013 witnessed the launch of a further companion journal *Digital Journalism* to provide a site for scholarly discussion, analysis and responses to the wide ranging implications of digital technologies for the practice and study of journalism. From the outset, the publication of themed issues has been a commitment for all journals. Their purpose is first, to focus on highly significant or neglected areas of the field; second, to facilitate discussion and analysis of important and topical policy issues; and third, to offer readers an especially high quality and closely focused set of essays, analyses and discussions.

The *Journalism Studies: Theory and Practice* book series draws on a wide range of these themed issues from all journals and thereby extends the critical and public forum provided by them. The Editor of the journals works closely with guest editors to ensure that the books achieve relevance for readers and the highest standards of research rigour and academic excellence. The series makes a significant contribution to the field of journalism studies by inviting distinguished scholars, academics and journalism practitioners to discuss and debate the central concerns within the field. It also reaches a wider readership of scholars, students and practitioners across the social sciences, humanities and communication arts, encouraging them to engage critically with, but also to interrogate, the specialist scholarly studies of journalism which this series provides.

Cross-continental Views on Journalistic Skills

Edited by

Leen d'Haenens, Michaël Opgenhaffen and Maarten Corten

Routledge
Taylor & Francis Group
LONDON AND NEW YORK

First published 2014
by Routledge

Published 2014 by Routledge
2 Park Square, Milton Park, Abingdon, Oxfordshire OX14 4RN

and by Routledge
711 Third Avenue, New York, NY 10017

Routledge is an imprint of the Taylor and Francis Group, an informa business

First issued in paperback 2015

British Library Cataloguing in Publication Data
A catalogue record for this book is available from the British Library

ISBN 978-0-415-73491-2 (hbk)
ISBN 978-1-138-95382-6 (pbk)

Typeset in Helvetica
by Taylor & Francis Books

Publisher's Note
The publisher accepts responsibility for any inconsistencies that may have arisen during the conversion of this book from journal articles to book chapters, namely the possible inclusion of journal terminology.

Disclaimer
Every effort has been made to contact copyright holders for their permission to reprint material in this book. The publishers would be grateful to hear from any copyright holder who is not here acknowledged and will undertake to rectify any errors or omissions in future editions of this book.

Contents

Citation Information

The chapters in this book were originally published in *Journalism Practice*, volume 7, issue 2 (April 2013). When citing this material, please use the original page numbering for each article, as follows:

Editorial Note

Editorial Note
Bob Franklin
Journalism Practice, volume 7, issue 2 (April 2013)
pp. 123

Chapter 1

Introduction: Cross-continental views on journalistic skills in the digital age
Leen d'Haenens, Michaël Opgenhaffen, and Maarten Corten
Journalism Practice, volume 7, issue 2 (April 2013)
pp. 124–126

Chapter 2

Journalistic Tools of the Trade in Flanders: Is there a fit between journalism education and professional practice?
Michaël Opgenhaffen, Leen d'Haenens, and Maarten Corten
Journalism Practice, volume 7, issue 2 (April 2013)
pp. 127–144

Chapter 3

Beacons of Reliability: European journalism students and professionals on future qualifications for journalists
Nico Drok
Journalism Practice, volume 7, issue 2 (April 2013)
pp. 145–162

Chapter 4

The Global Journalist in the Twenty-First Century: A cross-national study of journalistic competencies
Lars Willnat, David H. Weaver, and Jihyang Choi
Journalism Practice, volume 7, issue 2 (April 2013)
pp. 163–183

Chapter 5

Culture Clash: International media training and the difficult adoption of Western journalism practices among Indonesian radio journalists
Nurhaya Muchtar and Thomas Hanitzsch
Journalism Practice, volume 7, issue 2 (April 2013)
pp. 184–198

Chapter 6

Investigative Journalism on Campus: The Australian experience
Ian Richards and Beate Josephi
Journalism Practice, volume 7, issue 2 (April 2013)
pp. 199–211

Chapter 7

Beyond Skills Training: Six macro themes in South African journalism education
Pieter J. Fourie
Journalism Practice, volume 7, issue 2 (April 2013)
pp. 212–230

Please direct any queries you may have about the citations to clsuk.permissions@cengage.com

Notes on Contributors

Jihyang Choi is a doctoral student in the School of Journalism at Indiana University. Before starting this doctoral program, she worked as a journalist at the *Hankookilbo*, a national newspaper in Seoul, South Korea. She holds a bachelor's degree in history from Yonsei University in Seoul and a master's degree in journalism from Indiana University.

Maarten Corten was a Teaching Assistant in Communication Science at the Institute for Media Studies, KU Leuven, Belgium, from 2010 until 2012. Together with Michaël Opgenhaffen and Leen d'Haenens, he is the co-author of *Nieuwsvaardig, een cross-mediale competentiematrix voor journalisten* (Leuven, 2011).

Leen d'Haenens is Professor in Communication Science at the Institute for Media Studies, KU Leuven, Belgium, where she teaches Media and Diversity, Western Media Policy, and Analysis of Media Texts. Her current research interests include cross-national news frame analyses of the Euro-crisis, Islam and Muslims, the study of commercial and public service broadcasters' diversity potential, and the study of power relations and alliances with regard to issues relevant to the multicultural society in mainstream and online media (ethnic discussion forums, blogs) in North-Western Europe.

Nico Drok is Professor of Media & Civil Society at Windesheim University of Applied Science, Zwolle, The Netherlands. He has been leader of the European Competence Profile Project of the European Journalism Training Association (EJTA), from 2005 until present. The EJTA survey was hosted by the Institut für Angewandte Medienwissenschaft of the ZHAW in Winterthur and analyzed by Carmen Koch and Vinzenz in cooperation with the author. His article is a revised and extended version of a paper that was presented at the IAMCR conference in Istanbul. He is the author of *Bakens van Betrouwbaarheid* (Christelijke Hogeschool Windesheim, 2011).

Pieter J. Fourie is Professor Emeritus of Communication Science at the University of South Africa, where he was the Head of the Communication Sciences Department for 17 years. A former President of the South African Communication Association, he is the editor-in-chief of *Communication: South African Journal for Communication Theory and Research* and the author of a number of books and articles in the field of media studies.

Thomas Hanitzsch is Professor of Communication at the Institute of Communication Studies and Media Research, Ludwig Maximilians University, Munich. A former journalist, his teaching and research focus on global journalism cultures, war coverage, celebrity news and comparative methodology. He is the editor-in-chief of *Communication Theory*, and has authored and edited six books, including *The Handbook of Journalism Studies*

(Routledge, 2009, with Karin Wahl-Jorgensen) and *The Handbook of Comparative Communication Research* (Routledge, 2012, with Frank Esser). He is currently leading the Worlds of Journalism Study, a multinational survey of journalists (see www.worldsofjournalisms.org).

Beate Josephi is Coursework Masters Coordinator in the School of Communications and Arts at Edith Cowan University, Perth, Western Australia. She is a member of the Executive Committee of the International Association for Media and Communication Research (IAMCR). Her publications include the edited volume, *Journalism Education in Countries with Limited Media Freedom* (2010), as well as chapters in numerous international volumes. Her articles have appeared in journals such as *Journalism*, *The International Communication Gazette*, *Global Media and Communication*, *Australian Journalism Review* and *Communications: The European Journal for Communication Research*.

Nurhaya Muchtar is Assistant Professor in the Department of Communications Media at Indiana University of Pennsylvania. Dr. Muchtar's research interests focus on communication and media development, journalism practice and intercultural communication. She has presented her research primarily through the Broadcasting Educator Association (BEA) and the International Communication Association (ICA). Her research has appeared in the *Journal of Communications Media*. Prior to her academic career, she worked as a media training coordinator and training consultant for international media training organizations in Indonesia.

Michaël Opgenhaffen is Assistant Professor at the Institute for Media Studies, KU Leuven, Belgium, and at the University of Leiden, The Netherlands. He teaches New Media and Society and Social Media Research in the master's programs in Journalism. His research focuses on the use of social media in journalism practice, on the changing nature of journalism, and on the possible mismatches between journalism education and journalism practice.

Ian Richards is Professor of Journalism at the University of South Australia in Adelaide and is an Australian Research Council (ARC) "Expert of International Standing". He has twice been appointed to the national Humanities and Creative Arts Research Evaluation Committee as part of the Australian Government's ERA (Excellence in Research Australia) exercise which is designed to assess research quality within Australia's higher education institutions. He has been editor of *Australian Journalism Review* since 2003, and is on the editorial board of five international journalism journals. His publications include *Quagmires and Quandaries: Exploring Journalism Ethics* (2005) and chapters in a range of books.

David H. Weaver is Distinguished Professor Emeritus and the former Roy W. Howard Research Professor in the School of Journalism at Indiana University-Bloomington, where he has served on the faculty since receiving his PhD in Mass Communication Research from the University of North Carolina at Chapel Hill in 1974. His teaching and research interests have focused on studies of journalists, media agenda setting, voter learning from news media, foreign news coverage, and newspaper readership. He has published a dozen books on these subjects, as well as many articles and chapters. He is a past President of AEJMC and MAPOR, and a Fellow of ICA.

Lars Willnat is Professor in the School of Journalism at Indiana University. Before joining Indiana University in 2009, Professor Willnat taught at the George Washington University in Washington, DC, and at the Chinese University of Hong Kong. His teaching and research interests include media effects on political attitudes, theoretical aspects of public opinion formation, and international communication. He received his PhD in Mass Communication from Indiana University in 1992.

PREFACE

As the editors of this issue of *Journalism Practice* announce in their opening line, "you are reading a special issue . . . focused on precisely what it means to be a professional journalist today and in the near future in terms of the journalistic competencies necessary to work as a journalist". The urgency for such a focus is obvious given the remarkable technological, economic and audience-related changes which are refashioning all aspects of journalism practice and, in turn, prompting reconsideration of the relevant requirements for journalism education and training. Significantly, the editors are also concerned to address any "possible mismatches between journalism practice, on the one hand, and journalism studies and education, on the other". And because these changes in journalism are evident globally, the editors have gathered contributions from Europe, South-East Asia, Australia, South Africa and across the globe to ensure an inclusive and well-rounded discussion.

I congratulate guest editors Leen d'Haenens, Michaël Opgenhaffen and Maarten Corten for bringing together such a distinguished group of scholars and experienced teachers to discuss the very important question about how best to equip journalists with the skills, knowledge and competencies necessary to sustain and reinvigorate the profession of journalism. I also wish to record my gratitude to the reviewers—Professor Tim Luckhurst, Kent University, UK; Dr Gunnar Nygren, Sodertorn University, Sweden; and Professor Karen Sanders, University of San Pablo, Madrid—who read and commented on earlier drafts of all the papers published in this issue.

BOB FRANKLIN
Editor

INTRODUCTION
Cross-continental views on journalistic skills in the digital age

Leen d'Haenens, Michaël Opgenhaffen, and **Maarten Corten**

You are reading a special issue of *Journalism Practice* (Volume 7, Number 2) focused on precisely what it means to be a professional journalist today and in the near future in terms of the journalistic competencies necessary to work as a journalist. Journalism practice has changed rapidly and dramatically in the first decade of the twenty-first century. Digitization has placed considerable pressures on conventional business models, transformed the news production process and redefined the relationship between newsmakers and their audiences. Professional journalism, moreover, has lost its monopoly of news reflecting the impact of the internet, citizen journalism and social media. Unfortunately, news media and professional journalists have reacted rather late to these new technological, economic and audience-specific realities, the major obstacles hampering innovation in the press being its very structure as well as the professional culture that has long dominated the sector. Publishers continue to focus on the production and distribution of a physical newspaper, and this focus is also characteristic of the culture of the sector. There is a strong fear of cannibalization, a very marked feeling of competition and there are few contacts with players outside the newspaper's own field.

Undoubtedly one of the alarming drawbacks is that professional journalism might be considered as indefinable or even obsolete, in times when the value of journalistic products and accurate reporting remain as important as ever. Journalists and editors indeed produce added value by revealing interrelations in the daily deluge of news facts and information, by sketching the background to stories and by checking facts. The readers' appetite for news and background information has not diminished. What has changed, however, is the way in which people absorb journalism content.

We wonder how journalists can cope with these changes and show resilience by turning risks into opportunities, by examining which skills in newsgathering and news production are important, and what personality traits are necessary to work within a (cross-media) news organization. Journalists' accommodation to change entails, among other things, producing distinctive journalistic products, working online within a multi-channel strategy, involving users in experiments, looking for ways to stop the culture of the free availability of content on the net, and more generally, exploring new models in co-operation with parties from outside the press industry.

The aim of this special issue is to map cross-national answers (by way of research conducted in different continents) to the numerous challenges of the digital age. By understanding the changing nature of journalism practice with a focus on the contemporary and future skills needed, we hope not only to describe the ways in which recent evolutions affect journalism practitioners in different regions throughout the world, but also to address the possible mismatches between journalism practice, on the one hand, and journalism studies and journalism education, on the other. These insights are meant to describe the ways in which recent evolutions have changed journalism throughout the world, but also to provide in-depth information on how professional and novitiate or starting journalists can mark their positions and even reclaim their professional status now and in the next decade by incorporating new ways of news reporting (e.g., through crowd-funding, creative storytelling, efficient uses of social media, data-driven journalism and/or hyperlocal journalism).

The introductory essay provides a cross-media competency matrix by way of a methodology to study both general and specific journalistic competencies in order to test the match (or lack thereof) with journalism education and scholarship. Subsequent contributions review the current state of research about journalistic competencies in different continents (Europe, South-East Asia, Australia and South Africa) and more generally across the globe. Each region-specific contribution deals with a region-relevant topic: the feasibility of a pan-European journalistic competency profile against global trends in the journalistic profession; the competencies needed for functioning "on the ground" in complex multi-ethnic and multi-religious Indonesia; the position of investigative journalism in Australia; the impact of macro themes such as race, gender, development, indigenization and new media in South Africa's journalism education.

Spanning a regional variety that goes beyond the usual North Atlantic zone, this special issue presents contributions by experts in journalism studies. Each article offers findings on journalistic competencies in different geographical and cultural areas, paying attention to recent and future technological, cultural and economic evolutions in journalism that ask for new journalistic skills and attitudes, and addressing the possible mismatch between journalism practice, on the one hand, and journalism education and research, on the other.

In their essay "Journalistic Tools of the Trade in Flanders", Michaël Opgenhaffen, Leen d'Haenens and Maarten Corten investigate the (mis)match between the needs of Flemish professional journalism, on the one hand, and Flemish journalism curricula, on the other. Through a survey of 600 professional journalists, competencies that are considered necessary for the job are mapped in a so-called journalistic competency matrix. This snapshot provides us with a relatively monomedia or serial monomedia journalistic profile and a sector that does not ask for far-reaching, medium-specific specialization. In parallel, professional and academic journalism education programs are analyzed. Both types of findings are put together to identify the degree of congruence (or lack of it) between the professional field and the journalism educational programs on offer. Although educational curricula and their media-wide study programs seem to prepare aspiring journalists to a serial monomedia career sufficiently, there are a number of striking discrepancies between the sector and journalism education with respect to topical focus.

Commissioned by the European Journalism Training Association (EJTA), Nico Drok draws together Europe-wide views on future qualifications for journalists among journalism professionals and future professionals. Shifts expected in the qualification profile and in the views of important stakeholders are assessed. Drok's research shows a high level of consensus between students and professionals when it comes to the 50 qualifications in the European profile. A "back to basics" strategy is put forward in an attempt to face current turbulence in the journalistic field. The author concludes that perhaps European schools of journalism, and by extension journalism schools around the globe, should switch from a "follower" to an "innovator" mode.

Lars Willnat, David Weaver and Jihyang Choi go cross-national in their contribution focused on the global journalist in the twenty-first century, taking on the complicated task of looking for general patterns and trends in journalistic competencies, and thereby selecting findings from surveys of about 29,000 journalists working in 31 countries or territories, conducted between 1996 and 2011. The authors do not observe clear worldwide patterns of such competencies, except for a tendency in some countries for younger, less experienced, less formally educated journalists, lacking the necessary multimedia skills, who do not value highly the interpretive or analytical role of journalism, and consequently feel less work-related freedom and satisfaction.

Moving on to South-East Asia, and particularly to multi-ethnic and multi-religious Indonesia, Thomas Hanitzsch and Nurhaya Muchtar address the challenges that face international media education/donor agencies that have been offering media training in Indonesia in an effort to improve democracy and civil society. Indonesian (radio) journalists identify incompatibilities between the normative underpinnings in the Western training materials used and the context in which journalism practice is conducted in Indonesia. Complex situations "on the ground" tend to hamper training effectiveness and the adoption of news skills and knowledge substantially.

Staying in the same geographical area, Ian Richards and Beate Josephi document the strong presence of investigative journalism in the journalism programs of Australian universities, delivering journalism graduates who have the skills and understanding necessary to conduct serious investigative work; thus positively impacting on the overall quality of Australia's journalistic output. Notwithstanding this key responsibility that journalism schools take on, the wider context within which universities are operating currently puts a lot of pressure on journalism education.

Finally, concluding this *tour d'horizons*, Pieter Fourie argues convincingly that journalism education is always embedded in the socio-cultural and political realities of the society it covers. Hence, issues of race, gender, identity, development and democracy are paramount in South African journalism theory and discourse about journalism skills.

JOURNALISTIC TOOLS OF THE TRADE IN FLANDERS

Is there a fit between journalism education and professional practice?

Michaël Opgenhaffen, Leen d'Haenens, and **Maarten Corten**

This research is based on two observations. First, journalism practice has changed rapidly and dramatically in the first decade of the twenty-first century. Digitization has imposed pressures on conventional business models, transformed the news production process, and redefined the relationship between newsmakers and their audiences. Second, during that same period Flemish journalism education has boomed, resulting in as many as six professional Bachelor's programs and three academic Master's programs in journalism. These parallel developments have led us to investigate the (mis)match between the needs of Flemish professional journalism, on the one hand, and the ambitions of Flemish journalism curricula, on the other. To this end a survey was distributed among 600 professional journalists to map the competencies they feel are required for the job. Linking these competencies to specific media profiles enabled us to assess the relative importance of each item within a specific working context. Then all Flemish professional and academic journalism education programs were analyzed based on topic focus and media platform. The findings of these investigations were aggregated in an effort to identify the degree of congruence (or lack of it) between the professional field and the educational programs on offer.

Introduction

Considering the numerous changes journalism practice has experienced across the last 10–15 years, the rather abstract concept of *digital revolution* quickly comes to mind when looking for common ground. Digitization has radically changed the context in which journalists and news organizations operate. Business models must make accommodations to shifting income flows, while journalists seem to be losing their grip on their traditional gatekeeping roles. News-gathering practices have also changed, introducing computer-assisted research (CAR) and source-checking tools—not to mention social media—to the newsroom. Digitization has also made it possible for news organizations to merge different media platforms into one single newsroom. Individual journalists become "multimedia journalists", and online journalists are able to compose news messages consisting of a variety of modalities. With this in mind, we shall briefly discuss the context and characteristics of news gathering and production in contemporary journalism.

Competition

Since the arrival of the internet as a publication platform, news organizations have struggled to stay afloat since the classic business model no longer guarantees financial health in the face of a boundless space where spreading content of all sorts and kinds is both cheap and instantaneous. But while marketers and individual advertisers quickly and massively turn to online advertising, news organizations fail to connect online with their former "business associates": marketers promoted their product through new players such as Google and news aggregators (Edmonds 2009; Scott 2005; *The Economist* 2010). Classifieds found their way to Craigslist and the like, and job adverts were decimated as the 2008 recession kicked in (Pew 2010). As a result, advertising revenues in print publications dropped sharply. The loss could not be recouped through cheap online advertising because of low effectiveness and ad avoidance as cheapening factors. Furthermore, offline readership dropped to an all-time low following the 2008 recession (Edmonds, Guskin, and Rosenstiel 2011).

News organizations, particularly those specializing in print publications, were faced with a financial deficit and many businesses closed, not least those which were fully dependent on advertising revenue such as the free newspapers (Debackere 2010). In order to survive, businesses applied different strategies, mostly resulting in a smaller, more flexible newsroom. Across the world journalists were laid off, monomedia newsrooms turned into multimedia centers and journalists were introduced to multimedia journalism. Nowadays, the number of permanent "staffer" appointments is dropping while free-lancing is on the rise. Image management, networking and knowledge of the media landscape have become standard competencies (Deuze and Fortunati 2011). Although such changes have been presented as innovations, critical voices state that these innovations share one common goal: producing more output with fewer resources. The well-known study by Nick Davies illustrates this statement: he found that nowadays, journalists produce three times the content their colleagues produced in 1985 (Davies 2009). In a multimedia environment this does not necessarily mean that journalists produce a literal three-fold increase in unique content, but that they publish roughly the same content more frequently across different media platforms (Avilés and Carvajal 2008; Buijs 2008). Consequently, journalists have less and less time to devote to news gathering, which forces them to let go of such journalistic standards as reliability and content diversity (Buijs 2008; Franklin 2011). Aspiring journalists should be aware that in many cases their working environment will not be conducive to any "ideal" notion of journalism. Also work stress and burn-out are on the rise according to Flemish research (a series of in-depth interviews by Teugels et al. 2011). As a result, stress coping skills will probably rise in perceived importance as well.

In addition to decreased job security, today's journalists are forced to position themselves against new information sources, not least the expansive army of bloggers (Singer 2011). However, claiming that journalists have completely lost their gatekeeping function may be a gross exaggeration. First of all, the average internet user only turns to a limited number of sources in order to keep up with current events (Purcell et al. 2010). Indeed, it seems that the competent, so-called "digital native" is far from taking full advantage of the wealth of information available online nor does (s)he apply advanced methods to unlock this information (Brotcorne, Mertens, and Valenduc 2009). In other words, journalists as gatekeepers have not disappeared; rather they have turned into *information managers*, filtering, structuring and contextualizing content (Hermans et al.

2009). Specific competencies may be required to fulfil this new task in a world of bloggers, citizen journalists, commenters and proactive news users.

News Gathering

A changing, digital world implies changing news-gathering skills, mostly relying on CAR. Generally speaking, this online research practice can be divided into two tracks: search strategies, fact checking and searching for additional information, on the one hand, and an analytical process that includes data scraping, data screening and data analysis, on the other hand. Specific search strategies are needed to find information on the internet and to check it for reliability. However, these competencies do not seem to grow automatically on the job. In all, online searching skills among journalists tend to be of mediocre quality, as demonstrated by Machill and Beiler in 2009 when they asked a number of journalists to go through an exercise in searching skills. Journalists mostly use online applications such as e-mail, websites and search engines, especially Google. Use of blogs, discussion boards, Usenet threads or RSS feeds is much less frequent (Hermans et al. 2009; Van Heeswijk 2007). It appears that journalists would benefit from specific search strategy training in order to be able to find information more efficiently and make better use of online platforms and tools. Attitudes to online news gathering are moderately positive, but journalists are concerned about the quality of information they can find on the internet (Fortunati et al. 2009). However, researchers state that in this time and age it has never been easier to access primary sources (Paulussen 2007). It is not just a matter of learning skills, so it seems, but also one of changing attitudes toward online news gathering. Again, specific training is one way to deal with this discrepancy.

Another way to search for online information (or rather, to search online for information) is to scan social media. Efficient use of social media can lead to topical and local information (Dersjant 2010) and usability standards in data-analytical software have greatly improved (Paulussen 2007), enabling journalists to analyze and visualize large data sets. Websites present tips and tricks to use their network for news gathering: e.g., Facebook for journalists or Twitter for newsrooms. Adding geographical information (e.g., via Foursquare) journalists can locate reliable sources or even witnesses to a newsworthy event. Again, a prerequisite to efficient use of social media is a "social media mindset" (Grimm 2010). However, research suggests that such a social media approach has been gaining ground very slowly and that few news companies have made significant inroads in key new digital areas such as mobile and social media. Most news organizations have a social media presence but seem at a loss concerning how these platforms might let them gather, verify and present the news, or interact with the audience. Studies have found that news outlets merely use social media platforms as a strategic and tactical promotional tool, ignoring the interactivity potential with Twitter followers, for instance (e.g., Greer and Ferguson 2011). A study of the 2011 Twitter feeds of 13 major US news organizations showed that the great majority of tweets promoted the organizations' own work and websites: no fewer than 93 percent of tweets on mainstream Twitter news feeds contained a link that bounced traffic back to the home site. Only 2 percent of tweets asked followers for information, either to flesh out a story or to provide feedback (Pew Research Center 2011). In Belgium, only a small minority of journalists are really convinced about the benefits of a "social media watch" (Quadrant Communications 2010). International research claims that in 2009 only half of the world's journalists used social networks in their news gathering (McClure and Middleberg 2009)—a percentage that may be skewed by an overrepresentation of American journalists. Similarly, US financial journalists do not think much of social networks, stating that they are of no use for news gathering today (Lariscy et al. 2009). According to a recent study, Dutch journalists lack time to make full use of social media (Hermans, Vergeer, and Pleijter 2011). These numbers are in sharp contrast with the opportunities social media offer journalists. In addition, many news organizations seem to struggle with their social media policy. In 2012, for example, Sky News issued a restrictive Twitter policy for its reporters, telling them not to retweet other people's tweets, to avoid personal or non-job subjects on their work accounts, and to check with the news desk in case of breaking news stories (Halliday 2012). All told, it can be argued that traditional news organizations lack the insight and techniques needed to make innovative and interactive use of digital social platforms.

News Production

In addition to working context and news-gathering practices, digitization has a profound effect on news production and distribution. Although the paradigm of "the multimedia animal" is rapidly losing support (Russial 2009), contemporary journalists probably benefit from a certain degree of multimedia flexibility (Dupagne and Garrison 2006). A key factor affecting the set of required news production competencies is the type of media convergence a news organization has undergone. As discussed earlier, news companies turned to media convergence in order to cut spending and to deliver news more efficiently, which implies that any given message is repurposed for multimedia distribution. Media convergence comes in different forms and intensities. Three modalities can be derived from the literature: intensity, locus of news production and affected production unit. To define intensity, one can turn to a model by Dailey (Dailey, Demo, and Spillman 2005) in which different stages of media convergence form a "convergence continuum". The outer left category on the continuum is cross-promotion, meaning that products of the collaborating newsroom or organization are only promoted as opposed to repurposed. Moving to the outer right side of the continuum, we pass stages involving copying content and sharing (journalistic or financial) resources. At the final stage, labelled "convergence", news organizations are completely converged into one news flow. Although insightful for our three-way typology, the major weakness of this model lies in its goal. Dailey et al. state that the final convergence stage is the one and only goal in media convergence, while news organizations might well be more comfortable with an intermediate stage such as cloning or cross-promotion. A second modality is the locus of news production, referring to the production phase in which convergence takes place, namely news gathering, news production or news distribution (Avilés and Carvajal 2008). Newsrooms can choose to collaborate in the news-gathering phase while still working autonomously in production and distribution. Journalists working for the Flemish public broadcaster share content intensely during the news-gathering phase, while news production and distribution are still conducted in specialized newsrooms (Musschoot and Lombaerts 2008). The third modality covers the production unit affected by the media convergence at the journalist, news team, newsroom and news brand levels (Opgenhaffen, Corten, and d'Haenens 2011). When a journalist single-handedly produces content for different media platforms, it can be said that intensive convergence covering all production phases takes place at the level of the individual journalist. However, a more common practice is to set up multimedia news teams in which journalists share journalistic and financial resources, after which each journalist produces content for one media platform. In this case, while intensive convergence in the news-gathering phase does take place at the individual's level, in the production and distribution phases such intensive convergence is located at the news team level. Taking into account these modalities, media convergence can have a different effect on required competencies for a rookie or experienced journalist.

Avilés and Carvajal (2008) identify two main media convergence models: the cross-media model and the integrated model, the former signaling a moderate convergence in the news-gathering phase at the newsroom level, the latter referring to intensive convergence covering the entire workflow at the level of the individual journalist. Although media convergence has often been vaunted as being the model of future journalism, implementation seems mostly limited to a cross-media model (Russial 2009; Domingo and Salaverria 2007). As far as the competencies required of a contemporary journalist are concerned, knowledge of CMS, mastering different media logics and different modalities (as in written text, video, photography, etc.) (Opgenhaffen, Corten, and d'Haenens 2011), repurposing and prepurposing skills (Avilés and Carvajal 2008) as well as team skills (Russial 2009; Dupagne and Garrison 2006) seem to have gained importance during the last decade.

Finally, the digital revolution has given birth to an entirely different animal: the online journalist. This new profile has a rather atypical workflow in comparison to that of offline colleagues. Online news allows implementation of a variety of modalities. However, this does not imply specialized multimedia competencies. Although knowledge of HTML, photo-editing software, CMS and even Flash may be relevant, general writing skills still tend to be more important (Steensen 2009; Thurman and Lupton 2008; Chung 2007; Magee 2005). That being said, online journalists need to adjust to the reality of online narratives, integrating multimedia elements, hyperlinks and interactive tools (Opgenhaffen 2009). We may be faced with what might be termed the "online paradox"—online journalists having to implement "new" modalities into their news narratives without needing specialized competencies, mainly thanks to the usability of software applications.

Research Questions

The profound changes journalism has undergone give rise to questions concerning the interaction (or lack of it) between the professional field and journalism education. The proliferation of educational programs in journalism is being viewed with an increasingly critical eye (Van Es and Van der Meulen 2010). Concerns are raised about the possible saturation of the market and the quality of such programs. In Flanders too, congruence between journalism education and practice is a hot topic. During the 1990s there was a boom in journalism education, with six Bachelor's and three Master's programs on offer. The current Flemish Minister of Media acknowledges the need for evidence-based journalistic quality and the need for clustering and specialization within journalism research (Lieten 2010).

The present study[1] aims to answer the following research questions addressed to the professional field:

RQ1: Which (combinations of) media platforms do Flemish journalists work for, and can different media profiles be identified based on their regularly produced output?

RQ2: Which competencies are important for beginner/starting journalists in relation to their media profile?

Regarding journalism curricula, the following research questions were asked:

RQ3: Which topic/subject emphases are implemented in the Bachelor's and Master's programs?

RQ4: How prominent are different media platforms in the Bachelor's and Master's programs?

Topic similarities and compatibility between the two fields were assessed and the prominence of the various media platforms in both the journalism sector and the curricula was mapped out. These findings support conclusions as to the degree of congruence between journalistic practice and the educational system.

Results

The Working Field of the Professional Journalist

An investigation was conducted among Flemish journalists to map out the required so-called "starting competencies". The goal of this study was to enable heads of journalism education programs to adjust their curricula, based on the research findings, to the requirements of the working field, if deemed necessary or useful. These research results, however, are not directly related to the available courses. After all, our analysis focuses on the competencies required by the sector and is therefore blind to individual curricula. Nico Drok (whose work can also be found in this special issue) conducted similar research, entitled "The European Competence Profile Project" (Drok 2010). Embedded in the European Journalism Training Association, this European project also seeks to connect education and practice through a set of required competencies.

In a first phase, 24 experts were interviewed in order to develop a list of competencies. Experts with different backgrounds needed to be interviewed to ensure the list was sufficiently inclusive. Consequently, 20 editors, editorial staff and editors-in-chief of different media brands and media platforms were asked to present their views on required competencies, reflecting on their own professional context. Additionally, four researchers with different expertise reflected on the future of journalistic practice. Fifty competencies were drawn from the transcripts of 24 in-depth interviews. A number of extra competencies were added based on literature review and topics covered in Flemish journalism curricula. The final list contained 57 competencies. Subsequently, an online questionnaire was sent to 2387 Flemish journalists, making use of the list of members of the General Association of Journalists in Belgium [Algemene Vereniging van Beroepsjournalisten in België (AVBB)] and the Association of Journalists of the Periodical Press [Vereniging van de Journalisten van de Periodieke Pers (VJPP)]. In addition, a Web link to the survey was published on the website of the AVBB, the website of the Pascal Decroos Fund (a non-profit organization funding investigative journalism) and the newsletter of

Journalinks.be. These extra publication channels were intended to reach journalists who are not registered in the aforementioned databases, such as freelancers. In total, 597 journalists took part in the survey, reflecting a response rate of 25 percent. Taking into account the busy schedule of journalists and the many invitations they receive to participate in academic research, the response rate can be considered satisfactory. In order to answer the first research question, respondents were asked to determine their media profile. To this end, journalists could tick off media platforms for which they produce media content. They could choose between "print", "radio", "television" and "Web"; "mobile" was not included as a media platform. Both Web and print platforms include a number of publication types: print, for example, can be split into newspapers and periodicals; Web is a collection of sub-media such as Web pages, RSS feeds, discussion platforms, etc. (Opgenhaffen 2009). Based on these options, 14 unique media profiles arose from the data. In view of further analyses, such as the linking to the competency list, the more "lightly populated" media profiles were combined so that seven robust media profiles remained, as listed in Table 1.

Adding up the frequencies of the four single or monomedia profiles (print, television, radio and Web), a majority of the respondents (73 percent) label themselves as monomedia journalists. Taking into account other data from the survey, the multimedia profile "print–Web" can also be categorized as monomedial. This profile mainly consists of print journalists who occasionally repurpose a text for online publication. Although writing for the Web requires specific skills, print–Web journalists do not deal in specific online characteristics such as multimediality, interactivity and hypertextuality. In summary, almost 9 out of 10 Flemish journalists produce content for a single media platform only. The majority work for the printed press; only 5 percent of the respondents exclusively produce online content. The multimedia profiles were clustered in order to avoid further fragmentation when carrying out more in-depth analysis. Six percent work for both radio and television, possibly in relation with a third media platform. Seven percent work in other multimedia combinations. Having determined their media profile, respondents could then indicate which modalities—the sensory building blocks of a news item, so to speak—they regularly call on in their news coverage. "Regularly" supposed both regularity and familiarity with the modality used. "Use" implied that the respondents need not have developed any given modality themselves. In other words, online journalists can indicate the use of video in their coverage regardless of authorship (e.g., YouTube videos, etc.). Table 2 shows the percentage of journalists regularly using the listed modalities within each media profile.

TABLE 1
Percentage of journalists per media profile ($N=597$)

Media profile	%
Print	36.01
TV	21.44
Print–Web	13.74
Radio	10.05
Radio–TV +	6.37
Web	5.36
Rest	7.04
Total	100

TABLE 2
Percentage of journalists per media profile using each modality regularly ($N=597$)

	Print	Print–Web	Web	Radio	Radio–TV +	TV	Rest
Written text	97.1	94.7	96.7	72.4	86.5	55.7	92.5
Photographs	73.1	84.2	90.0	1.7	37.8	37.7	60.0
Video	3.4	22.4	86.7	8.6	56.8	95.1	60.0
Illustrations	41.8	47.4	46.7	0.0	18.9	33.6	20.0
Info-graphs	43.8	47.4	23.3	3.4	27.0	43.4	12.5
Spoken text	3.3	7.9	36.7	100.0	73.0	80.3	80.0
Non-verbal sound	0.0	3.9	3.3	77.6	37.8	50.0	40.0
Music	0.5	2.6	6.7	62.1	32.4	59.0	52.5
Animation video	0.5	0.0	10.0	0.0	21.6	39.3	15.0

The "written text" modality is a constant for a majority of the journalists within each media profile. When comparing modalities across the different media profiles, three tendencies are to be distinguished. The "print" and "print–Web" profiles are very much alike, sharing such static modalities as written text, pictures, illustrations and info-graphs. This finding reinforces the notion that print–Web journalists are in fact print journalists who occasionally supply content to an online platform. Secondly, a more dynamic group can be distinguished, encompassing television, radio and the radio–TV+ profile and whose members mostly engage in audiovisual modalities. Finally, the "Web" profile bears close resemblance to the static profiles, while making more use of video and spoken text. It seems that journalists in Flanders not only conduct predominantly single or monomedia production of news, but also make use of the available modalities in a rather monomedia fashion.

However, some distinctions are worth stressing. Firstly, the results are only related to news production and news distribution. These data do not allow for statements concerning news gathering and the use of different media. Secondly, this is a snapshot which leads us to the conclusion that journalists mainly work for one media platform at a time. However, a number of researchers involved in the qualitative part of our study have warned of increasingly unpredictable career paths. More and more, a journalistic career will develop in a "serial monomedia" fashion, with journalists alternating between different media platforms. Multimedia flexibility may thus become a major competency within such a context.

The third research question concerns the competencies required for beginner or starting journalists, as perceived by professionals. In the online survey, respondents were asked to rate on five-point Likert scales the importance of the 57 competencies identified through the interviews with the expert, where 1 stood for "not important at all" and 5 for "very important". In the first round, journalists were asked to assess the importance of each competence based on their personal situation; in a second round they had to assess the competencies from the perspective of an inexperienced, beginner journalist. In both rounds, it was stressed that the competencies must be assessed within their own "media environment", which led back to the media profile drawn by the journalist at the outset of the questionnaire. This method allows for differentiation of the perceived importance of the 57 competencies over different media profiles. These competencies are then clustered into three categories: attitudes and personality, news gathering, and news production. A general overview of the 57 competencies is provided in the competency matrix in Appendix A. This matrix can be used in journalism schools to evaluate their curricula, as has already been done in Flanders. In the discussion we will elaborate on this further. In what follows, the three categories are discussed separately. Table 3 supplies the scores of the competencies belonging to the "attitudes and personality" category. All scores discussed in this study reflect the assessments from the perspective of a starting journalist.

Competencies in this category are generally rated highly. Competencies such as being studious, accurate and critical are seen as indispensable. Also general knowledge obtains a high score, a lot higher even than specialized knowledge. Strikingly these scores apply to all media. In other words, an ANOVA test did not reveal any difference per competency among the scores of the different media profiles. Variables such as employer type do not yield significant variations. In other words, there is great consensus on the value of these competencies.

In Table 4, we find that foreign-language knowledge such as knowledge of French and English is considered very important for news gathering, while remarkably, command of the German language—Belgium's third national language after Dutch and French—is valued much less. The sector gives high scores to traditional news-gathering techniques such as networking, interviewing techniques, and the offline study of source material, while CAR techniques and use of new media—except for online search strategies—are all seen as less important. Concerning the use of offline and online news-gathering channels, there is a significant gap between Web profile and other media profiles. Online journalists value skills such as networking ($F(6,477) = 3.73$; $p < 0.001$), interviewing techniques ($F(6,381) = 3.15$; $p < 0.05$) and offline news gathering ($F(6,478) = 5.72$; $p < 0.001$) to a much lesser degree than do their colleagues, while naming search engine ($F(6,478) = 4.01$; $p < 0.001$) and social media ($F(6,477) = 4.56$; $p < 0.001$) use as crucial. These findings reinforce the impression that online journalists mostly use the internet to gather information or create content. Based on the required skills, telephone interviews

TABLE 3

Importance of competencies for a starting journalist: attitudes and personal features ($N = 498$)

Skills	Score
Inquisitiveness	4.85
Curiosity	4.73
Accuracy	4.66
Criticalness	4.58
Handle stress and deadlines well	4.55
Handle criticism well	4.55
Be passionate	4.47
Have broad general knowledge	4.38
Have good social skills	4.18
Be a team player	4.15
Assertive behavior	4.13
Be acquainted with journalistic ethics	3.87
Knowledge of other cultures	3.37
Want to profile yourself within the journalistic sector	3.20
Understand the media landscape	2.97
Be familiar with copyright	2.86
Specialist knowledge about one theme	2.84
Be aware of techniques in PR and communication management	2.79
Have knowledge of the different statutes according to which a journalist can work	2.68
Have knowledge of commercial aspects of a media company	2.55
Be a team leader	2.26

TABLE 4
Importance of competencies for a starting journalist: news gathering ($N=485$)

Skills	Score
Command of English	4.17
Analyze and synthesize large amounts of information	4.11
Network, make contacts	4.02
Command of French	4.00
Search online information on an advanced level	3.98
Master interview techniques	3.93
Search for news and check sources without the use of the internet	3.90
Look at news in a historic perspective	3.69
Consult archives	3.60
Interpret statistical data and graphics	3.40
Make use of social network sites (Facebook, Twitter, etc.)	2.96
Interpret academic publications	2.96
Command of German	2.87
Know about the publicness of state legislation	2.80
Command another foreign language	2.78
Make use of the Office-package on an advanced level	2.42
Conduct polls	2.14

and fieldwork do not seem to belong to the range of duties of the online journalist (Paulussen and Raeymaeckers 2010).

News production competencies, listed in Table 5, in general receive a lower score than those related to news gathering and attitudes and personality. Strikingly, the three most important competencies involve language skills. Moreover, language skills are rated highly across all media profiles, unlike the other news production competencies. Depending on the media profile, specific news production skills are viewed as more

TABLE 5
Importance of competencies for a starting journalist: news production ($N=475$)

Skills	Score
Have a fluent style of writing	4.60
Write flawlessly	4.50
Master different text styles and argumentations	4.24
Think and work audience-directed	3.89
Speaking skills (articulation, diction, etc.)	3.51
Adapt writing for online publications	3.23
Have a feeling for lay-out and user-friendliness	3.08
Knowledge of functioning and logic of different media platforms	3.06
Versatility as to different media platforms	3.05
Be specialized in one medium	2.46
Audio recording (equipment, volume, background noise, etc.)	2.37
Audio editing	2.36
Working with HTML	2.28
Video editing	2.11
Photography (equipment, composition, light, etc.)	2.09
Film (equipment, image, sound, etc.)	2.02
Moderate discussion forums or reactions	1.97
Touch up photographs (Photoshop, etc.)	1.91
Work with authoring software (Publisher, Dreamweaver, etc.)	1.84

important, even though they are rarely awarded an above-average score. Based on these assessments, the Flemish online journalist hardly qualifies as a specialized "multimedia editor'. After all, none of the news production skills are labeled as very important by journalists with a Web profile. It should be added also that multimedia flexibility (mean = 3.06) is seen as more important than media-specific specialization (mean = 2.46). These findings reinforce the idea of the serial monomedial career, during which journalists work for one media platform at a time, but come into contact with different media platforms throughout their career.

Journalism Curricula

One interesting way to use these results is to compare them with the learning goals as formulated within journalism curricula. The current research focuses on existing higher education[2] programs. Additional education programs, "Bachelor-after-Bachelor's" programs, continuing education, evening classes, etc., are not included. Objective information on the Bachelor's and Master's programs can be found through the Europe-wide ECTS (European Credit Transfer System) descriptions.[3] These ECTS descriptions can be consulted online for each course. They have two main advantages. Firstly, the formulated objectives, content and study material give an accurate image of what the course has to offer and whether that content is applied to a single media platform, to multiple platforms or to no specific platform. Secondly, the information on the intended workload makes it possible to determine, for each program, the amount of study time that is allocated to the various topical emphases and media platforms. In May 2010 the online ECTS descriptions of Flanders' six Bachelor's and three Master's programs in journalism (2009–2010 Academic Year) were analyzed. As elective courses, they invariably adopted a similar approach or learning goal, one slot was reserved for each set of elective courses. Each Bachelor's program totaled 180 credits, with each Master's program totaling 60 credits. Within each program, every ECTS file was awarded two labels. The first label addresses the topic focus:

- News gathering (both traditional news gathering and CAR).
- News production (technique and format).
- Internship and project (news gathering and news production put to practice).
- Journalism and communication (formulation of theories).
- General education (social studies).
- Command of language.
- Command of foreign languages.
- ICT (Office and online applications).
- Journalism ethics.

This list of categories is intended to be as exhaustive as possible, so as to allow comparison with the research results derived from the journalism sector.

The second label addresses the media orientation of a given course:

- Encompassing all media—no special emphasis on a specific platform.
- Print.
- Television.
- Radio.
- Web.

- Elective media platform: students choose the platform.
- Multimedia, tackling different media platforms simultaneously.

A final category is divided into a clustered and integrated multimedia approach. A clustered multimedia course deals with different media platforms separately or serially, while an integrated multimedia course emphasizes the specific multimedia working context in which various media platforms interact. After assigning two labels to each course, we determined the frequency of each category within the Flemish Bachelor's and Master's programs. Figure 1 shows the percentage for each content category within the Bachelor's and Master's programs. It should be noted that the total of the Bachelor's and Master's levels amounts to 100 percent. In other words, both the Bachelor's programs—amounting to 180 credits—and the Master's programs—60 credits—are recalculated to a percentage. As we do not intend to compare the individual programs among themselves, Figure 1 presents an overview of the results.

Education in journalism and communication studies' theory is part of the core Flemish Master's curricula. No study time is reserved for general knowledge in a specific course. This is to be expected as candidate students have already graduated from a Bachelor's program, a Master's program or a professional Bachelor's program followed by a preparatory program. The Flemish Master's programs in journalism do not offer foreign-language courses. Since the three Master's programs are offered by departments of applied linguistics where sufficient multilingual expertise is at hand, this lack may seem rather puzzling. By way of comparison, the Bachelor's programs do provide study time for both multilingual and general education. However, attention in the Master's programs is mainly directed at news production and traineeship. Journalism ethics, command of language, ICT and the gathering of information tend to receive only limited attention in both the Bachelor's and Master's programs.

Their varying objectives notwithstanding, the Bachelor's and Master's programs treat media platforms in similar ways (Figure 2). A majority of courses do not focus on one specific media platform, covering instead media-wide and media-blind topics. Compulsory monomedia courses are scarce. A focus on print shows up more often, although this mainly concerns command of written language, an obviously useful competency on other media platforms as well. A lot of study time is allocated to medium-specific specialization,

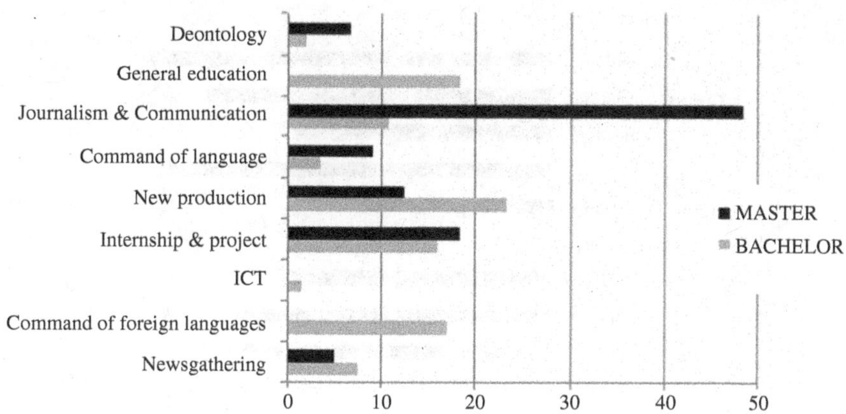

FIGURE 1

Topic emphases in Flemish Bachelor's and Master's curricula (%)

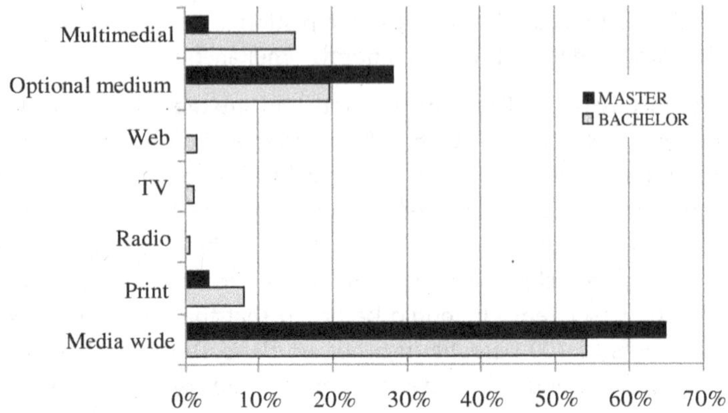

FIGURE 2
Prominence of media platforms in Flemish Bachelor's and Master's programs (%)

as indicated by the high percentage in the optional medium category. The Bachelor's program distinguishes itself from the Master's program in the multimedia offer. It should be mentioned that this multimedia supply mainly consists of clustered courses (80 percent), with a significantly smaller integrated course component (20 percent).

Conclusions

Our central research question concerned the fit (or lack of fit) between journalistic practice and journalism education programs in Flanders. Figure 3 is based on research into the journalism sector: the scores for the 57 competencies are clustered in categories that were used in the analysis of the ECTS descriptions. This data approach allows for a cautious comparison between required competencies as perceived by the sector and topic emphases in the educational system. A first assessment identifies a rather large gap with respect to news production skills.

While Bachelor's and, to a lesser degree, Master's programs strongly focus on news production and traineeship, these are not perceived as high priorities for a starting

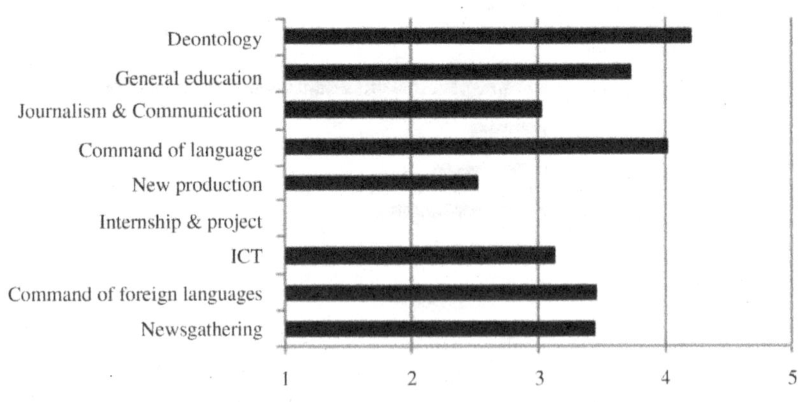

FIGURE 3
Importance of competencies for a starting journalist ($N = 475$)

journalist by the journalism sector. Conversely, journalism ethics, general knowledge, command of language, multilingualism and information-gathering skills are highly valued by the sector but rather neglected in the curricula. The absence of multilingual education as part of the Master's programs is cause for concern. The focus on journalistic theory is also noticeably high in the Master's programs, at least compared to the needs expressed by the journalism sector. General knowledge seems to be experienced as a lack by graduated Bachelors, while assuming a prominent spot in the education supply. According to the expert interviews, the general education of the Bachelor's graduates is often seen as inadequate. The demand for academically trained journalists is constantly growing. Furthermore, the limited time devoted to news-gathering skills in the curricula is incongruent with the perceived importance of these competencies for a starting journalist. A comparison of the media orientation of both the journalism sector and the curricula highlights similar issues, we see more parallel foci. The sector does not ask for far-reaching, medium-specific specialization. This snapshot provides us with a relatively monomedia image, although it is expected that journalistic careers will increasingly unfold in a more "serial monomedia" fashion. Both the Bachelor's and Master's programs in Flanders respond well to this overall trend. All Bachelor's programs show more or less the same structure whereby students get general, media-blind content in the first year. In the second year, students are introduced into different media platforms. In the third year they choose one platform in which they specialize. As such, Bachelor's programs combine medium-specific specialization with multimedia flexibility. The Master's programs prepare the students for a serial monomedia career through a general journalistic education, complemented with an emphasis on a specific modality (e.g., written text), serving as a "multimedia basis". In summary, both the journalism sector and the curricula display a parallel media orientation, although there remain a number of discrepancies content-wise between the perceived importance of journalistic skills by the sector and the journalistic education courses, as could be derived from the ECTS descriptions.

Other than academic insight on the congruence (or lack thereof) between journalistic practice and journalism education, this study also provides the latter with a concrete curricula evaluation tool in relation to the preferences of the sector, on the one hand, and educational goals and self-perceived role in the broad journalistic field, on the other hand. As a matter of fact, one higher education institution, in setting up a Bachelor's program in journalism, has already carried out such an evaluation based on the aforementioned results and actually changed its curriculum to fit the needs of the journalism sector better. The program is now tailored to prepare students more intensively to a serial monomedia career and a moderately converged newsroom, giving them a better understanding of the different media platforms and their specific media logics. While the original program only dealt with online practice as a third-year specialization, the new version includes online production courses as part of the core curriculum. Also, instead of introducing every second-year student to every media platform, this (shortened) introduction is now part of the first-year curriculum. Then, in the second year, students select a major and a minor media platform, which involves creating content as part of multimedia news teams. In other words, medium specialization is now being combined with cross-media insights. Possibly more use will be made of our competency matrix (see Appendix A), as journalism programs have been undergoing a process of thorough assessment in the Netherlands and Flanders.

The question remains whether there is sufficient correspondence between the professional field of journalism and journalism education. While education curricula and their media-wide study programs seem to prepare aspiring journalists for a serial monomedia career, there are a number of striking discrepancies between the sector and journalism education with respect to topic focus. Given such discrepancies, the question concerning the degree to which mutual correspondence is desirable becomes unavoidable. While curricula do not need to reflect the perceived needs of the sector exactly, they can strive to be a force for innovation. Although the journalism sector does not set much store by knowledge of the media landscape, entrepreneurship and computer-assisted reporting skills, educational institutions may well choose to continue to pay attention to these topics. Hence, the last word belongs to department heads whose job it is to determine, in collaboration with the teaching staff, whether the current programs achieve their stated goals. Ongoing dialogue between the sector and alumni can be a valuable instrument for regular adjustment.

NOTES

1. This article was part of a research project funded by the Educational Development Fund of the KU Leuven Association. This fund subsidizes projects aimed at educational improvement and innovation.
2. The six professional Bachelor's programs are run by Arteveldehogeschool, Erasmushogeschool Brussels, Hogeschool West-Vlaanderen, Lessius Mechelen, Plantijn Hogeschool Antwerp and Xios Hogeschool Limburg; the three Master's programs are part of Erasmushogeschool Brussels, Hogeschool-Universiteit Brussels and Lessius University College Antwerp. There is no distinction between Master's programs at universities and university colleges in Flanders. The Master's programs at university colleges will be "integrated" in the University Association by October 2013.
3. In the ECTS system, for each course, a description containing information on objectives, content, study material and work load (expressed in ECTS) is developed. This facilitates inter-institutional comparison across Europe.

REFERENCES

Avilés, Jose Alberto Garcia, and Miguel Carvajal. 2008. "Integrated and Cross-media Newsroom Convergence: Two Models of Multimedia News Production: The Cases of Novotécnica and La Verdad Multimedia in Spain." *Convergence: The International Journal of Research into New Media Technologies* 14 (2): 221–239.

Brotcorne, Perine, Luc Mertens, and Gerard Valenduc. 2009. *Les jeunes off-line et la fracture numérique. Les risques d'inégalités dans la génération des 'natifs numeriques'*. Namur: Fondation travail-Université ASBL.

Buijs, Kees. 2008. *Journalistieke kwaliteit in het crossmediale tijdperk*. The Hague: Boom Onderwijs.

Chung, Deborah Soun. 2007. "Profits and Perils: Online News Producers' Perceptions of Interactivity and Uses of Interactive Features." *Convergence* 13 (1): 43–61.

Dailey, Larry, Lory Demo, and Mary Spillman. 2005. "The Convergence Continuum: A Model for Studying Collaboration between Media Newsrooms." *Atlantic Journal of Communication* 13 (3): 150–168.

Davies, Nick. 2009. *Flat Earth News*. New York: Random House.

Debackere, Jan. 2010. "Grote schoonmaak bij gratis kranten." *De Morgen*, February 19.

Dersjant, Theo. 2010. "Richtlijnen voor de omgang met sociale media." http://www.denieuwere porter.nl/2010/03/richtlijnen-reuters-voor-omgang-met-sociale-media/.

Deuze, Mark, and Leonardo Fortunati. 2011. "Atypical News Work, Atypical Media Management." In *Managing Media Work*, edited by Mark Deuze, 111–120. Thousand Oaks, CA: Sage.

Domingo, David, and Ramon Salaverria. 2007. *Four Dimensions of Journalistic Convergence: A Preliminary Approach to Current Media Trends in Spain*. Austin: University of Texas at Austin.

Drok, Nico. 2010. "The European Competence Profile Project." Paper presented at the World Journalism Education Congress, South Africa, July 27.

Dupagne, Michel, and Bruce Garrison. 2006. "The Meaning and Influence of Convergence: A Qualitative Case Study of Newsroom Work at the Tampa News Center." *Journalism Studies* 7 (2): 237–255.

Edmonds, Rick. 2009. "FTC Testimony Explains 3 Trends for Newspapers in 2010." http://www.poynter.org/column.asp?id=123&aid=174173.

Edmonds, Rick, Emily Guskin, and Tom Rosenstiel. 2011. *Newspapers: By the numbers. The State of the News Media 2011*. http://stateofthemedia.org/2011/newspapers-essay/data-page-6/.

Fortunati, Leopoldina, Mauro Sarrica, John O'Sullivan, Aukse Balčytienė, Halliki Harro-Loit, Phil Macgregor, Nayia Roussou, Ramón Salaverría, and Federico De Luca. 2009. "The Influence of the Internet on European Journalism." *Journal of Computer-mediated Communication* 14: 928–963.

Franklin, Bob. 2011. "Sources, Credibility and the Continuing Crisis of UK Journalism." In *Journalists, Sources and Credibility; New Perspectives*, edited by Bob Franklin and Matt Carlson, 90–106. New York: Routledge.

Greer, Clark F., and Douglas A. Ferguson. 2011. "Using Twitter for Promotion and Branding: A Content Analysis of Local Television Twitter Sites." *Journal of Broadcasting and Electronic Media* 55 (2): 198–214.

Grimm, Joe. 2010. "The Social Media Skills You Need to Qualify for Journalism Jobs." http://www.poynter.org/column.asp?id=77&aid=177611.

Halliday, Josh. 2012. "Sky News clamps down on Twitter use." http://www.guardian.co.uk/media/2012/feb/07/sky-news-twitter-clampdown.

Hermans, Liesbeth, Maurice Vergeer, Leen d'Haenens, and Karolien Joniaux. 2009. "Journalistiek en internet in de lage landen. Een vergelijkende studie naar het internetgebruik van Nederlandse en Vlaamse journalisten." *Tijdschrift voor Communicatiewetenschap* 37 (2): 99–117.

Hermans, Liesbeth, Maurice Vergeer, and Alexander Pleijter. 2011. *Nederlandse journalisten in 2010*. Nijmegen: Radboud Universiteit Nijmegen.

Lariscy, Ruthan W., Elizabeth J. Avery, Kaye D. Sweetser, and Pauline Howes. 2009. "An Examination of the Role of Line Social Media in Journalists' Source Mix." *Public Relations Review* 35: 314–316.

Lieten, Ingrid. 2010. *Beleidsbrief Media 2010–2011*. Brussels: Flemish Government.

Machill, Marcel, and Markus Beiler. 2009. "The Importance of the Internet for Journalistic Research." *Journalism Studies* 10 (2): 178–203.

Magee, C. Max. 2005. "Roles of Journalists in Online Newsrooms." http://blog.ohmynews.com/dangun76/attachment/1260732429.pdf.

McClure, Jennifer, and Don Middleberg. 2009. *Key Findings of the 2009 Middleberg/SNCR Survey of Media in the Wired World*. San Jose, CA: Society for New Communication Research.

Musschoot, Iris, and Bart Lombaerts. 2008. *Media in beweging: handboek voor de professional*. Leuven: Lannoo Campus.

Opgenhaffen, Michael. 2009. "Multimedia, Interactivity, and Hypertext in Online News: Effect on News Processing and Objective and Subjective Knowledge". Unpublished doctoral dissertation, University of Leuven.

Opgenhaffen, Michael, Maarten Corten, and Leen d'Haenens. 2011. *Nieuwsvaardig: een crossmediale competentiematrix voor journalisten*. Leuven: Lannoo Campus.

Paulussen, Steve. 2007. "CAR als middel voor primaire journalistiek." *Tijdschrift voor Communicatiewetenschap* 35 (3): 19–31.

Paulussen, Steve, and Karin Raeymaeckers. 2010. *Journalisten. Profiel van een beroepsgroep*. Leuven: Lannoo Campus.

Pew Research Center. 2010. "The State of the News Media." http://stateofthemedia.org/2010/.

Pew Research Center. 2011. "How Mainstream Media Outlets Use Twitter." http://www.journalism.org/node/27311.

Purcell, Kristen, Lee Rainie, Mitchell Amie, Tom Rosenstiel, and Kenny Olmstead. 2010. "Understanding the Participatory News Consumer." http://www.pewinternet.org/Reports/2010/Online-News.aspx.

Quadrant Communications. 2010. "Het gebruik van sociale media bij Belgische journalisten." http://www.quadrantcommunications.be/blog/detail/pers_en_social_media/.

Russial, John. 2009. "Growth of Multimedia Not Extensive at Newspapers"." *Newspaper Research Journal* 30 (3): 58–74.

Scott, Ben. 2005. "A Contemporary History of Digital Journalism." *Television and New Media* 6 (1): 89–126.

Singer, Jane B. 2011. "Journalism in a Network." In *Managing Media Work*, edited by Mark Deuze, 103–110. Thousand Oaks, CA: Sage.

Steensen, Steen. 2009. "The shaping of an online feature journalist." *Journalism* 10 (5): 702–718.

Teugels, Marleen, Elke Van Hoof, and Hans De Witte. 2011. "Burnout bij journalisten in Vlaanderen: De slachtoffers van de nieuwsfabriek." *De journalist* 136: 6–8.

The Economist. 2010. "The strange survival of ink." http://www.economist.com/node/16322554.

Thurman, Neil, and Ben Lupton. 2008. "Convergence Calls: Multimedia Storytelling at British News Websites." *Convergence* 14 (4): 439–455.

Van Es, Ana, and Mark van der Meulen. 2010. "Te veel opleidingen journalistiek voor te weinig banen." http://www.volkskrant.nl/vk/nl/2694/Tech-Media/archief/article/detail/1041198/2010/10/28/Te-veel-opleidingen-journalistiek-voor-te-weinig-banen.dhtml.

Van Heeswijk, Eric. 2007. *Journalistiek en Internet 2002–2007: Technofielen of digibeten?* Apeldoorn: Het Spinhuis.

Appendix A

The Crossmedia Competency Matrix for Journalists

	Total	Print	Print + web	Web	Radio	Radio + TV + extra	TV	Multiple platforms
Attitudes and personal features	T	P	P-W	W	R	R-TV+	TV	MP
Being studious	5							
Being curious	5							
Being accurate	5							
Being critical	5							
Being able to cope with stress and time pressure	5							
Being able to cope with critique	5							
Being driven	4							
Having a broad, general knowledge	4							
Being social	4							
Being a teamplayer	4							
Being assertive	4							
Knowing journalistic deontology	4							
Having knowledge of different cultures	3							
Being willing to position yourself and to network	3							
Understanding the media landscape	3							
Being familiar with copyright	3							
Having expertise on a specific subject	3							
Being aware of PR and communication management	3							
Knowing the different statutes for a journalist	3							
Understanding the commercial aspects of a media	3							
Being a teamleader	2							
Total 'attitudes and personal features'	4							
Research	T	P	P-W	W	R	R-TV+	TV	MP
Mastering the English language	4							
Analyzing and synthesizing large amounts of information	4							
Networking	4			3				
Mastering the French language	4							
Searching online at an advanced level	4			5		3		
Mastering interview techniques	4			3				
Being to execute offline research	4			3				
Placing news in a historical perspective	4							
Consulting archives	4							
Interpreting statistical data and graphs	3							
Using social networksites	3			4				
Interpreting academic papers	3							
Mastering the German language	3							
Being familiar with freedom of information legislation	3							
Mastering another language	3							
Using Office software at an advanced level	2							
Composing polls	2							
Total 'research'	3							
News production	T	P	P-W	W	R	R-TV+	TV	MP
Writing fluently	5							
Writing flawlessly	5							
Mastering different forms of text structure and	4							
Being aware of your target audience	4							
Mastering verbal skills	4	3	3	3	5			5
Writing text for online	3		4	5				4
Being in touch with lay-out and usability	3		4	4				
Knowing the structure and logic of different media	3			4				
Being able to work for different media platforms	3			4				4
Being specialised in one media platform	2				3			
Recording audio	2	1			5	3	3	3
Editing audio	2	1	1		5	3	3	3
Mastering HTML	2		3	4				3
Editing video	2	1	1				4	3
Photographing	2				1			
Recording video	2						3	3
Moderating discussion boards or reactions	2			3				
Mastering authoring software	2			3				
Editing photos	2			4	1			
Total 'news production'	3	2						

BEACONS OF RELIABILITY

European journalism students and professionals on future qualifications for journalists[1]

Nico Drok

Journalism is changing rapidly. The professional routines that have been used so successfully in the past century seem less suitable for the future. This calls for a shift in the qualification profile European journalism schools use as a basis for their curricula. It is not easy to establish which qualifications will need more attention in future education provision or—because of the limited time budget of students and schools—which qualifications will have to manage with less attention as a result. The European Journalism Training Association (EJTA) has commissioned research into the views of European journalism professionals and future professionals. Which shifts in the European qualification profile do they anticipate and how (if at all) do these important stakeholders differ in their views? How do European students of journalism and European professional journalists assess qualifications that are related to major innovations in journalism? The research shows a high level of consensus among students and professionals concerning the shifts in relative weight of each of the 50 qualifications in the European profile. Furthermore, it turns out that both groups favour a "back to basics" strategy in these turbulent times. It appears that within this strategy there is enough room for two out of six innovations, but far less for the other four. These outcomes are valuable for journalism schools' intent on rethinking their curricula, but they do not solve the fundamental question: to what extent can or should education stay ahead of developments in the profession?

Introduction

The third iteration of the World Journalism Education Conference takes place in 2013 in Mechelen (Belgium), hot on the heels of the Singapore (2007) and Grahamstown (2010) editions. It will bring together practitioners, researchers, teachers and students from around the globe to discuss a variety of themes: freedom of the press, accountability, conflict reporting, media literacy, etc. The central theme for 2013 will revolve around the question: how can journalism education play a more decisive role in shaping the future of the profession? "Renewing journalism through education": the assumption behind this central theme is that journalism education can be perceived as a way "in which society can intervene to influence the development of journalism". Yet, questions about the role educators should play in making journalism better are "surprisingly rarely asked, but need to be addressed" (Curran 2005, xiv).

Over the years there have been numerous arguments about the nature of journalism and journalism education (Gaunt 1992; Splichal and Sparks 1994; Fröhlich and Holtz-Bacha

2003; Hanitzsch, Löffelholz, and Weaver 2005; de Burgh 2005; Josephi 2009; Franklin and Mensing 2011; Mensing 2011). What underlies this (global) debate is, according to Deuze (2006, 21), "the consensus among practitioners that the status quo in the industry is the ideal one, hence newcomers only need to internalize what their senior peers already do", while on the other hand scholars "tend to feel there is only one way of doing things—the academic way". The bulk of these discussions centre around four of the main dilemmas in European journalism schools: *concept* (should courses focus on journalism *stricto sensu*, or on everything that may be viewed as related to "the media"?); *expertise* (should journalism education favour practical skills or academic study?); *focus* (should the training be meant for current or future practice?); academic *mission* (should education be aimed at journalism as it is actually developing, or as we would wish it to develop?).

These dilemmas become even thornier with European journalism changing rapidly in quite fundamental ways. The success of European journalism in the twentieth century was based, among other things, on three foundations of the mass media model—scarcity of information, media monopoly and the presence of a mass audience. These foundations are eroding due to massive economic, technological and sociocultural changes (Küng, Picard, and Towse 2008; Bowman and Willis 2003; Halman, Sieben Inge, and van Zundert 2011; Bauman 2007). As Mensing observes,

> the practices of today were created during a time when information was scarce and distribution was generally one way through channels that had monopolistic advantages that no longer exist. Students now need to develop a different set of skills to deal with information abundance, network distribution, intense competition and a communication process that is interactive, asynchronous and nearly free. (2011, 80)

Changes in Journalism

It is not easy to chart clearly the many—sometimes contradictory—developments in European journalism (cf. Franklin 2011b). Journalism can be regarded as a professional process in which products are disseminated for the benefit of the public by one or more platforms. But every facet of the trade—public, process, product (content/form), platform and profession—has been changing almost beyond recognition. On the basis of an extended literature study, the following innovative trends were identified. They are formulated in a rather apodictic way, which does not mean they are not open for discussion.

First of all, the relationship between the profession and its public is changing. The public shows an increasing desire for *participation* (Singer et al. 2011). Citizens have a great deal and variety of knowledge and some of them appear to be eager to share this knowledge (Gillmor 2004; Rosen 2008). At the same time new technology—interactive internet, social media—keeps expanding opportunities for public involvement (Domingo et al. 2008), from citizen journalism via user-generated content to civic journalism (Ahva 2010; Nip 2006). As a result, it is in journalism's best interest to incorporate more contributions from the public into its daily routines (Carpentier and De Cleen 2008; OECD Working Party on the Information Economy 2007; Witschge 2012).

Next, in a world that is characterized by an abundance of information, a trustworthy, open working method is becoming a key to success. Uncovering the truth remains the chief characteristic of the journalistic process: "In the end, the discipline of verification is what separates journalism from entertainment, propaganda, fiction or art" (Kovach and Rosenstiel 2001, 71). However, conventional journalism's claim of being a bringer of objective truths is no longer tenable in a post-modern and multicultural society (Fuller 1996; Calcutt and Hammond 2011; Karlsson 2011). Efforts to establish an image of reliability should substitute the old tenet of objectivity with *transparency* (cf. Florini 2007; Phillips 2012, Eberwein et al. 2011; Hunter and Van Wassenhove 2010; Erbsen 2011; Lee-Wright, Philips, and Witschge 2012).

Furthermore, there is a lack of connection between everyday personal issues and the problems that occur at the level of government and society as a whole (Couldry, Livingstone, and Markham 2007; Schröder and Larsen 2009). Instead of the exception to the rule—after all what is news is precisely that which is extraordinary—the rule itself should be regarded more often (Luyendijk 2009). In addition to the classic watchdog role there is a need for a guide-dog that can help the citizen navigate through post-modern life. The role of gathering and quickly disseminating information becomes less important than that of analysing and contextualizing it (Weaver et al. 2007; Hermans and Vergeer 2011). For this *navigation* function to be effective, the information imparted must be reliable, it must meet the relevance/urgency requirement and preferably also be solution-orientated in order to afford the user a possibility of (re)action (Heikkilä, Kunelius, and Ahva 2011; Drok 2007; Rosenberry and St. John 2010).

In addition, with regard to the form of the product there is a growing need for variety in genres and the use of new narrative forms. In journalism, issues of attractiveness in format have been more or less neglected for a long time, unlike, for instance, in the entertainment sector. Fixed genres were the norm and were rarely discussed or renewed (cf. Bird and Dardenne 1997). "By following real characters, affected by and affecting a topic at hand, and portrayed in action, a writer may impart crucial information deeply and personally, as characters and settings and a "storyteller's voice" relate news to audiences' own experiences" (Kramer 2009, 1). Such *story-telling* elements as multiple layers in the story, multiple perspectives, tension and recognition stimulate the actual use of news stories (Costera Meijer 2009; Glasser 2000; Barnhurst and Mutz 1997) and should be incorporated more often into the daily routines.

Finally, present-day media users increasingly expect information to reach them through a variety of platforms that complement and reinforce one another and offer interaction possibilities (Huibers 2008). Such a *cross-media* concept demands of the journalist definite insights into the functional strengths, weaknesses, styles and routines of the various media (Fenton 2010; Bakker and Bakker 2011). Finally, the news business is no longer a sellers' but a buyers' market. This puts the price of journalistic information under pressure, to such an extent that the question arises as to whether quality journalism can maintain itself for a wide public in a commercial context or whether it will become a merit good[2] (Bardoel 2003). In the meantime the need for *entrepreneurial journalism* is growing. This goes further than knowing the practical aspects of freelancing. It includes flexibility, knowing the market and understanding the economic laws of the profession (Jarvis 2010; Hunter and Van Wassenhove 2010; Gillmor 2010; Caplan 2012).

In Table 1 the six facets of journalism and the main innovations for each are summarized. These innovations demand a shift in the qualification profile of the (starting) journalist. European journalism schools need to know which changes important stakeholders are expecting in the qualification profile for the coming years, and whether their expectations accord with the developments reported in the literature.

TABLE 1
Six facets and their major innovation

Concerns	Innovation	Description
I Public	Participation	Making use of user-generated content or knowledge, whether or not through social media or internet communities
II Process	Transparency	Guaranteeing accountability and a trustworthy, open working method
III Product content	Navigation	Offering a relevant and reliable content, whether or not through in-depth research, and putting it in a meaningful context
IV Product form	Storytelling	Using narratives in an attractive and user-friendly way to knit together fragmented observations to construct meanings
V Platform	Cross-media	Dividing content over different media in the most effective way while stimulating interaction
VI Professional context	Entrepreneurship	Being focused on innovation of product, process and platform for the benefit of the public with regard to the economics of the profession

The Competence Project

Against the background of these transformations the European Journalism Training Association (EJTA) started the so-called Competence Project in 2005. The EJTA unites 60 European schools/institutes of journalism from 25 different European countries. EJTA members can be divided into three main categories (cf. Fröhlich and Holtz-Bacha 2003; Terzis 2009):

1) Journalism training at the higher education level (Bachelor and/or Master) at a general university or university of applied science. About 65 per cent of the members fall within this category.
2) Journalism training in a mid-career institution. About 25 per cent of the members fall within this category.
3) Journalism training in a corporate context (media companies, etc.). About 10 per cent of the members fall into this category.

Of course there are many on-the-job training opportunities outside of EJTA, increasingly on the basis of a university degree in a field other than journalism (cf. Josephi 2009). And of course a statement that Deuze (2006, 31) meant globally holds true for Europe: "journalism education as a socializing agent is becoming increasingly powerful in today's media, as a vast majority of newcomers worldwide come to the job with some kind of training or education in journalism."

The EJTA is characterized by diversity on almost every level. Members come from different countries with differing educational cultures, media systems, political histories and cultural contexts, and they speak 20 different languages. In spite of this diversity, there is a full consensus about the mission of the association and its member schools:[3]

Members of the EJTA educate or train their students/participants based on the principle that journalists should serve the public by:

- providing insights into political, economic and sociocultural conditions;
- stimulating and strengthening democracy at all levels;

- stimulating and strengthening personal and institutional accountability;
- strengthening the possibilities for citizens to make informed choices in societal and personal contexts;

while

- feeling responsible for the freedom of expression;
- respecting the integrity of individuals;
- being critical of sources and independent of vested interests;
- using customary ethical standards.

Agreement on this mission was the starting point for the Competence Project which consisted of three steps:

1) Establish the 10 most important competences.
2) Establish the five most important qualifications for each competence.
3) Establish the relative weight of the 50 qualifications.

In this article the focus will be on the third step, after a short explanation of the first two.

Competences and Qualifications

The first step in the Competence Project was to organize a series of expert meetings in order to specify the most important journalistic competences for a starting professional. A "competence" represents a combination of knowledge, understanding, skills and professional attitude that is needed to accomplish an important professional task, according to the definition of the Tuning group of the European Union.[4] Out of the discussions came a competence profile consisting of 10 elements. The core of the profile is derived from a description of the most important professional tasks (the journalistic cycle; competences 2–7). This core is preceded by a reflective competence (no. 1) and followed by an evaluative competence (no. 8). The profile is completed by two organizational competences: cooperate in a team (no. 9) and working in a formal organization (no. 10).

After their education or training students possess the competence to:

1) *Reflect* on the societal role of and developments within journalism.
2) *Find* relevant issues and angles based on the public and production aims of a given medium/several media.
3) *Organize* and plan journalistic work.
4) *Gather* information swiftly, using customary news-gathering techniques and research methods.
5) *Select* the essential information.
6) *Structure* information in a journalistic manner.
7) *Present* information in appropriate language and an effective journalistic form.
8) *Evaluate* and account for journalistic work.
9) *Cooperate* in a team or an editorial setting.
10) *Work* in a professional media organization or as a freelancer.

The second step in the process was to formulate the five main qualifications for each of the 10 competences. A "qualification" or "learning outcome" defines what a learner is expected to know or be able to demonstrate after completion of a course of learning.[5] To work as intended, a qualification must be formulated unambiguously and hinge on one single requirement. After five rounds of debate it was decided that the qualification profile would contain the 50 qualifications shown in Table 2.

Research Questions

The qualification profile serves as the quality assurance framework among EJTA members and it helps stimulate student mobility.[6] But it also has its shortcomings. First, it does not stem from extensive academic analysis but from roundtable discussions between experts. This might make the process more open to chance, even though the final result was agreed upon by all EJTA members at a General Meeting. Secondly, the qualification profile is static and not weighted, which might seem to suggest that all qualifications are of equal importance, now as well as in the future.

Therefore EJTA decided to conduct mid-scale research among professional journalists, students, heads of schools and teachers. In this article the focus is on the first two groups. For the schools, students and professionals are the most important stakeholders, because they are the direct "customers" with respect to educational content and graduates, respectively. In the end they are not the ones that make the final decisions about the curricula, but their influence is growing within the quality assurance and accreditation systems across Europe. While journalism schools may well try to "renew journalism through education", their success is increasingly measured by the level of satisfaction their students display, as well as the jobs their graduates obtain (cf. Josephi 2009). In addition, it is interesting to compare these two groups on the assumption that students are far less influenced by the pressure of daily practice and therefore more open to change and innovation. After all, they are the ones that must bring new blood to the profession (Rosen 1999; Splichal and Sparks 1994).

The research should answer the following, interrelated questions:

RQ1: In the view of European students of journalism and European professional journalists, which qualifications for starting journalists are going to be the most and the least important in the coming 10 years?

RQ2: How do European students of journalism and European professional journalists assess qualifications that are related to six important innovations in journalism?

Method[7]

The point of departure in answering these questions is the qualification profile (Table 2). The 50 qualifications in this profile were incorporated in random order in an English-language online survey hosted and analysed by the Institut für Angewandte Medienwissenschaft of the ZHAW in Winterthur (EJTA/IAM 2010, 2012). All members of EJTA were asked to draw the attention of their students to this survey and see to it that the respondents were well spread across levels of education (Bachelor, Master) and years of study. A contact person in each country was asked to recruit more or less authoritative professional journalists—often editors in chief—from the print (45 per cent), broadcast (40 per cent), online (10 per cent) and other (5 per cent) sectors. This resulted in 1044 students and 360 professionals from the field (the distribution is given in Table 3), who in this article are regarded as two uniform groups without any further subdivisions.

TABLE 2
The qualification profile: 10 competences with 50 qualifications

1	**The competence to reflect on societal role**
1.1	Have a commitment to society
1.2	Have insight in the influence of journalism in society
1.3	Be able to develop a grounded view of journalism
1.4	Understand the values that underlie professional choices
1.5	Be able to reflect on a future career
2	**The competence to find relevant issues and angles**
2.1	Know current events
2.2	Know the characteristics of different media
2.3	Be able to determine the relevance of a subject for a specific audience
2.4	Be able to stimulate debate
2.5	Be able to discover newsworthy issues on the basis of in-depth research
3	**The competence to organize and plan journalistic work**
3.1	Be able to make a realistic work plan
3.2	Be able to work under time pressure
3.3	Be able to adjust to unforeseen situations
3.4	Be able to organize contributions from the public
3.5	Be able to work within budget limits
4	**The competence to gather information swiftly**
4.1	Have good general knowledge
4.2	Have a more specialized knowledge in a field
4.3	Be able to use all required sources effectively
4.4	Have the ability to balance the stories
4.5	Have the will to interact with the public
5	**The competence to select essential information**
5.1	Be able to distinguish between main and side issues
5.2	Be able to select information on the basis of reliability
5.3	Be able to interpret the selected information
5.4	Be able to select information in accordance with the genre
5.5	Be aware of the impact of your information on the public
6	**The competence to structure information in a journalistic manner**
6.1	Be able to use different types of narrative structures
6.2	Be able to fine-tune content and form
6.3	Be able to structure in accordance with the genre
6.4	Be able to structure on the basis of relevance
6.5	Be able use new media structuring techniques
7	**The competence to present information in an effective journalistic form**
7.1	Have an outstanding linguistic competence
7.2	Present information in combinations of words, sounds and images
7.3	Master the basics of layout
7.4	Be able to work with technical infrastructure
7.5	Be able to cooperate with technicians
8	**The competence to account for journalistic work**
8.1	Have a clear idea of the required quality of journalistic products
8.2	Be able to evaluate own work
8.3	Be willing to take criticism
8.4	Be able to take responsibility for the choices made during the process
8.5	Be able to take responsibility for the product
9	**The competence to cooperate in a team**
9.1	Have good social skills
9.2	Be reliable
9.3	Show initiative
9.4	Show insight in own strengths and weaknesses
9.5	Show insight in relations within a team

TABLE 2
(continued)

10	**The competence to be aware of own role in a media organization and as a freelancer**
10.1	Be able to present ideas convincingly
10.2	Know the rights and obligations within an organization
10.3	Know the market conditions
10.4	Be able to evaluate the editorial policy
10.5	Know the practical aspects of being a freelancer

All respondents were asked to assess the importance which each of the 50 qualifications would assume in the coming 10 years. Using a slider whose initial position was its middle point, the respondents could weigh the 50 qualifications on a scale from − − to + +. Moving the slider to the left meant the qualification in question was less important than the average, moving it to the right meant it was more important than the average. Under the visible scale was an invisible scale with a point distribution from 0 to 100. The actual scores were standardized with 0 as the average. Therefore the scale scores ranged from − 50 (= sharp decrease in relative importance) to + 50 (= sharp increase in relative importance).

To answer the second research question, the three most relevant qualifications for each of the six innovations were selected from the profile and their ranking scores were compared. Furthermore, a factor analysis was carried out to see if clusters of qualifications were present in the views of students and professionals and if they could be related to the six innovations. This did not lead to a satisfactory result: too many relevant variables had to be excluded in the process (see Appendix A), and the analysis results were not consistent for the two groups of respondents.

Results

The first research question was: "In the view of European students of journalism and European professional journalists which qualifications for starting journalists are going to be the most and the least important in the coming 10 years?"

The 10 top-ranked qualifications show a strong degree of consensus between students and professionals. Seven of the 50 qualifications are found in the top 10 of both groups of stakeholders (Table 4). There is even complete agreement about the top three: 9.2 ("be reliable"), 5.2 ("be able to select information on the basis of reliability") and 4.1 ("have good general knowledge"). The differences are limited and one group's top 10 qualifications are found within the other's top 15.

There also appears to be a high level of agreement between students and professionals about which qualifications will decrease in relative importance in the

TABLE 3
Respondents

	Students		Journalists	
	N	%	*N*	%
North (Denmark, Estonia, Finland, Lithuania, Sweden)	206	20	96	27
West (Belgium, France, Netherlands, United Kingdom)	425	41	76	21
Central (Austria, Germany, Switzerland)	92	9	76	21
East (Bulgaria, Czech Republic, Russia, Slovenia)	262	25	68	19
South (Albania, Macedonia, Spain)	59	6	44	12
Total	1044	100	360	100

TABLE 4
Top 10 qualifications (students/journalists)

Top 10—students	Students' ranking	Journalists' ranking	Difference
9.2 Be reliable	1	1	0
5.2 Be able to select information on the basis of reliability	2	2	0
4.1 Have good general knowledge	3	3	0
8.3 Be willing to take criticism	4	9	+5
3.2 Be able to work under time pressure	5	5	0
8.5 Be able to take responsibility for the product	6	10	+4
8.4 Be able to take responsibility for choices made during the process	7	12	+5
5.5 Be aware of the impact of your information on the public	8	14	+6
2.1 Know current events	9	8	−1
9.3 Show initiative	10	4	−6

coming decade (Table 5). The 10 qualifications scoring the lowest among students all fall within the journalists' 50–37 range, though often in different positions. It is not easy to find one common denominator for the 10 qualifications that score the lowest among students. A common thread is that students expect that working within a framework that limits creativity will become relatively less important in the next 10 years. Such a framework could be in the area of organization (3.5, 3.1) or genre and form (7.3, 6.3, 5.4). The influence of third parties such as technicians (7.5) and the public (3.4) could also limit creativity. Furthermore, students do not seem to have high expectations of particular forms of reflection (10.4, 1.5).

Generally speaking, it can be concluded that the differences between students and professionals are not great and not systematic. On the contrary: the level of consensus on the ranking of all 50 qualifications is rather high, with a ranking correlation (Spearman) of 0.8568. Both students and professionals place qualifications that might limit their

TABLE 5
Bottom 10 qualifications (students/journalists)

Bottom 10—students	Students' ranking	Journalists' ranking	Difference
3.1 Be able to make a realistic work plan	41	37	−4
5.4 Be able to select information in accordance with the genre	42	39	−3
7.5 Be able to cooperate with technicians	43	43	0
1.5 Be able to reflect on a future career	44	50	6
10.4 Be able to evaluate the editorial policy	45	46	1
6.3 Be able to structure in accordance with the genre	46	42	−4
10.3 Know the market conditions	47	47	0
7.3 Master the basics of layout	48	48	0
3.4 Be able to organize contributions from the public	49	45	−4
3.5 Be able to work within budget limits	50	40	−10

professional autonomy in the bottom 10, while stressing traditional core values—such as reliability, responsibility, analytical skills and the ability to work quickly—in their top 10.

The second research question was: "How do European students of journalism and European professional journalists assess qualifications that are related to six innovations in journalism?" The six innovations that have been singled out on the basis of literature are: participation, transparency, navigation, storytelling, cross-media work and entrepreneurship (Table 1). An overview of the ranking scores of the qualifications linked to these innovations is given in Figure 1. The assumption is that the ranking of those qualifications that are related to a given innovation gives us information about the respondent's view on the relative importance of that innovation.

As seen before, the overall differences between the two groups of respondents are relatively small. There is no clear evidence to suggest that students systematically have a more positive attitude towards the six innovations as compared to the professional journalists. Those qualifications related to an open working method (transparency) and to offering relevant content within a meaningful context (navigation) are ranked highest by both professionals and students. It seems that both groups of respondents realize that guiding your audience in an open and responsible way might be a key success factor in a world increasingly characterized by abundance of information and opinions.

The qualifications with the lowest ranking are found in the participation and entrepreneurial section. Both European students of journalism and European professional journalists rank below average the will to interact and the ability to stimulate debate. The ability to "organise contributions from the public"—which is at the very core of participation and co-creation—is found in the nether regions of the ranking. Students even rank this item lower than professionals do. Professionals and students differ in their assessment of the ability to adjust to unforeseen situations: the future journalists value this kind of flexibility much higher that their older peers. Both groups agree in their low ranking of the business side of entrepreneurial journalism: knowing market conditions and knowing the practical aspects of being a freelancer. The very low score given by professionals to future knowledge of the practical aspects of freelance work could be explained by the fact that there were very few freelancers among them. However, it is surprising that students also foresee a diminishing relative importance of this qualification, as a growing number of them will not be able to find steady employment and will have to make a living as self-employed journalists.

With regard to storytelling and cross-media work, the ranking is below average. Essential qualifications such as being able to use different types of narrative structures (storytelling) or knowing the characteristics of different media (cross-media) are ranked even lower by students than by professionals.

Conclusions

The first conclusion from our research is that the average level of consensus between professionals and students on the future weight of journalistic qualifications is high. Various studies have evidenced a definite convergence in their ideas of what constitute the essentials of journalism education, transcending various types of boundaries (Deuze 2006). Because our research—comparing the ways professionals and students view qualifications—is a first in Europe, we cannot determine whether the level of consensus between the two groups is growing or not. Furthermore, because of the

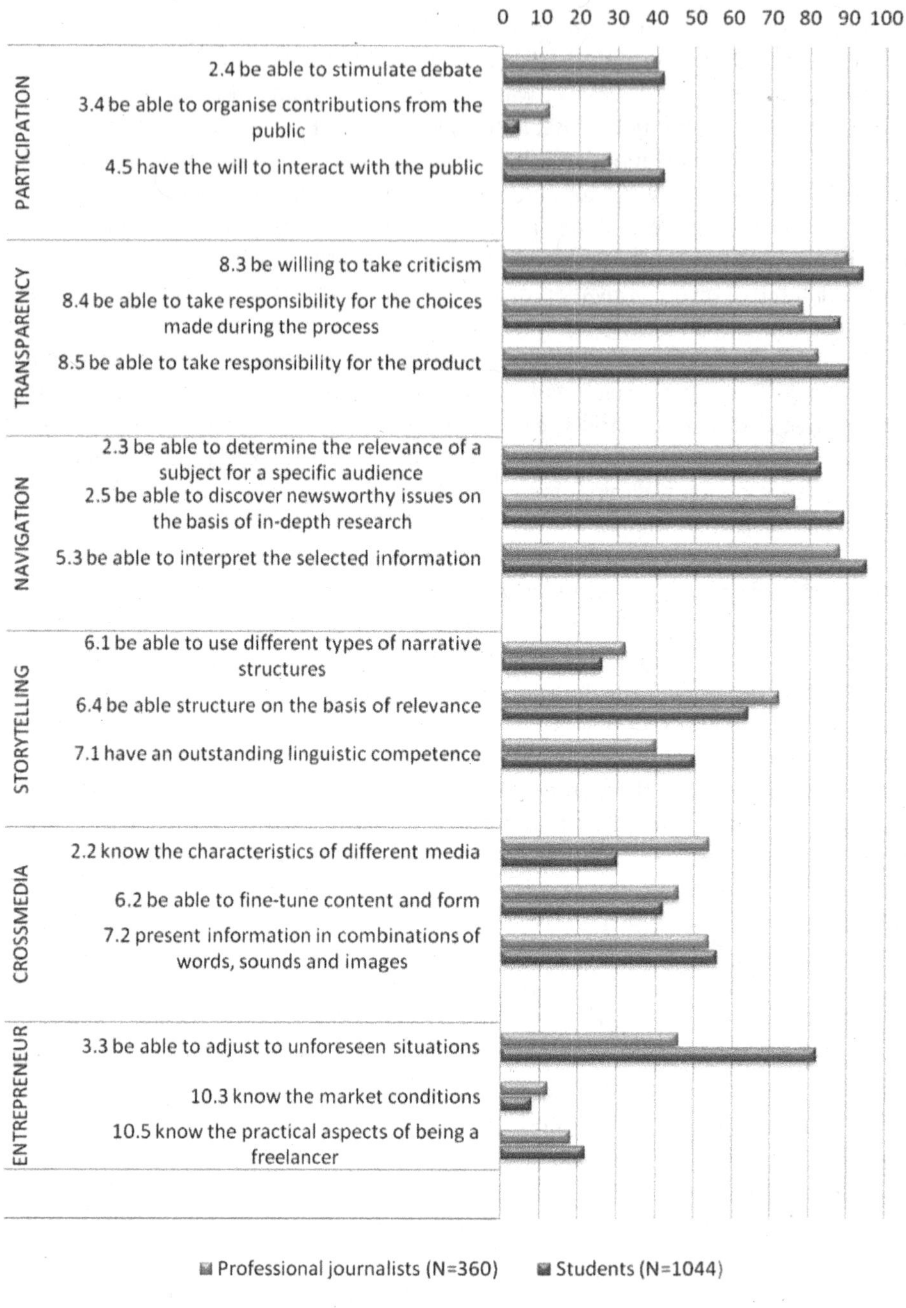

FIGURE 1
Ranking scores (1–100) on innovation-related qualifications (professionals/students)

scale of the research it is not possible to make a solid cross-national comparison. Therefore the tests that were run on the cross-national data (e.g., ANOVA) are not reported in this article, although they seem to corroborate the earlier findings of a consensus that surpasses boundaries based on nation, region or media system (Gaunt 1992; Splichal and Sparks 1994; Fröhlich and Holtz-Bacha 2003).

Second, if one asks students or professional journalists which parts of the journalistic qualification profile will increase in importance in the coming years, there is every chance that the answer will be: "everything". This research confirms that: in an absolute sense almost all qualifications are seen as becoming more important. However, not all qualifications are believed to gain importance to the same degree. There appears to be a clear order in the future importance of the 50 qualifications in the profile, and European students and professionals are in broad agreement over this. The qualifications that will increase most in importance can be placed under three main headings:

1) Reliability.
2) Sense of relevance and urgency.
3) Accountability.

Reliability concerns both the journalist (first place in the ranking) and the information (second place). Combined with the high score of qualifications that relate to accountability, this tends to evidence a strong sense among (future) journalists that in the twenty-first century professional journalism must set itself apart through credibility. In a sea of information and opinions, credible journalism hinges on trustworthiness and transparency, however difficult achieving such an ideal may be in present-day practice (cf. Davies 2008). A second conclusion is that in the view of (future) journalists, qualifications that relate to one of the central tasks of journalism—the dissemination of *relevant* news—will further increase in relative importance.

Looking at the bottom of the rankings, we see a variety of qualifications. Again, the professionals are in broad agreement with the students: seven out of the latter's lowest-ranked 10 qualifications are in the journalist's bottom 10, and the other three are in their bottom 15. This consensus seems to be based on a shared endeavour to gain autonomy. One may call professional journalists "those who tend to crave for only one thing: creative and editorial autonomy" (Deuze 2009). There is evidence that the new generation of journalists want such autonomy at least as much as established professionals. It seems that this has not changed over the past 20 years: Splichal and Sparks noted "in our students' conception of the role of the journalist, there is a strong tendency towards stressing autonomy from outside pressures that may influence journalists in the discharge of their informational functions" (1994, 186).

The notion that students may view the future with a more open mind because they are younger and less aware of constraints of everyday practice appears to be incorrect. Just like the professional journalists, they do not see the current crisis in journalism as a starting point for radical change, but rather an incentive to emphasize traditional core values.

The question remains whether stressing autonomy and traditional values does sufficient justice to the great changes currently taking place or about to take place in journalism (Lee-Wright, Philips, and Witschge 2012; Franklin 2011b; Curran 2010; Fuller 2010; Costera Meijer 2009; Drok 2011). Therefore the second research question aimed to assess a number of qualifications related to six major innovations in journalism. The conclusion is that two of these innovations get more than average support from both professionals and students: navigation and reliability. This reflects a gradual shift in role conception among journalists—a shift that has been in motion for some time (Weaver et al. 2007; Hermans and Vergeer 2011; Opgenhaffen, d'Haenens and Corten 2011): from speedy news hunter to beacon of reliability. Almost all qualifications that are related to the other four innovations—cross-media, storytelling, participation, entrepreneurial journalism—show a score below average. Participation and entrepreneurial journalism have the lowest scores, which again suggests that both professionals and students are keen on autonomy. They prefer to do their professional work without interference from market forces or the public. Heinonen's conclusion with respect to professional journalists appears to hold for their future colleagues too: "From the perspective of most journalism professionals, the public continues to be distinctively an audience for the media product—even if the relationship has more interactive features than before". Overall, students seem to share this "prevailing tendency . . . toward inertia or at least conservatism" (2011, 52).

Discussion

The academic value of EJTA's Competence Research is limited, primarily because of its relatively narrow scale. A replication of the research on a larger scale would allow for more solid cross-sectional comparisons as well as a longitudinal perspective. As they stand, the project's results are more useful for journalism practice and educational policy than they are for the academic study of journalism. Nevertheless, the conclusions lead to at least one question that might be of interest to everyone who is concerned about the future of journalism: what should we make of the emphasis that both professionals and students place on autonomy and "back to basic" values? Is that the best strategy in a period of turbulent change, or does it stand in the way of accepting a new journalism paradigm based on inclusiveness?

Furthermore, the Competence Project of the EJTA primarily has relevance for journalism educators and practitioners in *Europe*. But as "the changes and challenges facing journalism education around the world are largely similar" (Deuze 2006, 20), it might be useful in other parts of the world as well. The results can play a constructive role in the dialogue about future curricula between educators and the industry. They could be of particular benefit in global discussions on the mission of journalism education: should it be aimed at the status quo (= *is*), at an expected future (= *probably will be*) or at a desired future (= *should be*)?

What should be the position of journalism schools in this? Josephi (2009, 52) states that: "Journalism education, as increasingly provided by tertiary institutions around the world, is seen as a preparation for and a corrective to journalism." Journalism schools are considered to have a bad record as centres for professional renewal and innovation (Rosen 1999; Bierhoff and Schmidt 1997). Mensing and Franklin suggest that "one of the criticisms of established newsrooms *and* journalism education programs is that they can be rigid and resistant to significant change" (2011, 6). A major challenge for European schools of journalism, and perhaps all schools of journalism around the globe, is to switch from "follower" mode to "innovator" mode (cf. Deuze 2006). The 2013 World Journalism Education Conference, with its central theme—"Renewing journalism through education"—will be the perfect opportunity for professionals, students, educators and researchers to extensively discuss this challenge and breathe new life into a beautiful profession in crisis.

NOTES

1. This article is an altered and extended version of a paper that was presented at the IAMCR-conference in Istanbul (cf. Drok, 2012).

2. Goods of social importance that cannot be made available, or sufficiently available, without intervention of the government.
3. See http://www.ejta.eu/index.php/website/projects/.
4. See http://www.unideusto.org/tuningeu/competences.html.
5. See http://www.unideusto.org/tuningeu/competences.html.
6. See EJTA's Mobility Catalogue, http://www.ejta.eu/index.php/mc.
7. The research group consisted of Carmen Koch and Vinzenz Wyss, both attached to the Institute of Applied Media Studies of Zurich University of Applied Sciences in Winterthur (Switzerland). Nico Drok, attached to the Media Research Centre, Windesheim University in Zwolle (Netherlands), was project leader on behalf of EJTA.

REFERENCES

Ahva, Laura. 2010. *Making News with Citizens*. Tampere: Tampere University Press.

Bakker, Tom, and Piet Bakker. 2011. *Handboek Nieuwe Media*. Alphen aan de Rijn: Kluwer.

Bardoel, Jo. 2003. "Macht zonder verantwoordelijkheid?" Oration, Katholieke Universiteit Nijmegen, Nijmegen.

Barnhurst, Kevin G., and Diana Mutz. 1997. "American Journalism and the Decline in Event-centered Reporting." *Journal of Communication* 47: 27–53.

Bauman, Zygmunt. 2007. *Liquid Times: Living in an Age of Uncertainty*. Cambridge: Polity Press.

Bierhoff, Jan, and Mogens Schmidt, eds., 1997. *European Journalism Training in Transition*. Maastricht: European Journalism Centre.

Bird, S. Elizabeth, and Robert W. Dardenne. 1997. "Myth, Chronicle and Story: Exploring the Narrative Qualities of News." In *Social Meanings of News*, edited by Daniel E. Berkowitz, 333–350. Thousand Oaks, CA: Sage.

Bowman, Shayne, and Chris Willis. 2003. "We Media. How Audiences Are Shaping the Future of News and Information." http://www.hypergene.net/wemedia.

Calcutt, Andrew, and Philip Hammond. 2011. *Journalism Studies: A Critical Introduction*. London: Routledge.

Caplan, Jeremy. 2012. "Cheap and Useful Tools that Can Help Entrepreneurial Journalists Be More Efficient." http://www.poynter.org/.

Carpentier, Nico, and Benjamin De Cleen. 2008. *Participation and Media Production*. Newcastle, UK: Cambridge Scholars Publishing.

Costera Meijer, Irene. 2009. "Waardevole journalistiek. Kwaliteit van leven als normatief ijkpunt voor nieuwsmedia?" Oration, Free University, Amsterdam.

Couldry, Nick, Sonia Livingstone, and Tim Markham. 2007. *Media Consumption and Public Engagement: Beyond the Presumption of Attention*. Basingstoke, UK: Palgrave Macmillan.

Curran, James. 2005. "Foreword." In *Making Journalist*, edited by Hugo de Burgh, xi–xv. London: Routledge.

Curran, James. 2010. "Technology Foretold." In *New Media, Old News: Journalism and Democracy in the Digital Age*, edited by Natalie Fenton, 19–34. London: Sage.

Davies, Nick. 2008. *Flat Earth News: An Award Winning Reporter Exposes Falsehood, Distortion and Propaganda in the Global Media*. London: Random House.

de Burgh, Hugo, ed., 2005. *Making Journalist. Divers Models, Global Issues*. London: Routledge.

Deuze, Mark. 2006. "Global Journalism Education. A Conceptual Approach." *Journalism Studies* 7 (1): 19–34.

Deuze, Mark. 2009. "The People Formerly Known As the Employers." *Journalism Theory Practice and Criticism* 10 (3): 315–318.

Domingo, David, Thorsten Quandt, Ari Heinonen, Steve Paulussen, Jane B. Singer, and Marina Vujnovic. 2008. "Participatory Journalism Practices in the Media and Beyond." *Journalism Practice* 2 (3): 326–342.

Drok, Nico. 2007. *De toekomst van de journalistiek*. Amsterdam: Boom.

Drok, Nico. 2011. *Bakens van betrouwbaarheid. Een onderzoek naar verschuivende journalistieke kwalificaties*. Zwolle: TUZE/Windesheim.

Drok, Nico. 2012. "Towards New Goals in European Journalism Education." *Journal of Applied Journalism and Media Studies* 1 (1): 52–65.

Eberwein, Tobias, Suzanne Fenglers, Epp Lauk, and Tanja Leppik-Bork, eds., 2011. *Mapping Media Accountability—In Europe and Beyond*. Köln: Herbert von Halem Verlag.

EJTA/IAM (European Journalism Training Association/Institut für Angewandte Medienwissenschaft). 2010. *The Weighting of Different Journalistic Competences*. Research report by Carmen Koch and Vinzenz Wyss, in cooperation with Nico Drok. Maastricht and Winterthur: European Journalism Training Association/Institut für Angewandte Medienwissenschaft.

EJTA/IAM (European Journalism Training Association/Institut für Angewandte Medienwissenschaft). 2012. *The Weighting of Different Journalistic Competences. Phase III*. Research report by Carmen Koch and Vinzenz Wyss, in cooperation with Nico Drok. Maastricht and Winterthur: European Journalism Training Association/Institut für Angewandte Medienwissenschaft.

Erbsen, Claude E. 2011. "Transparency." In *Innovations in Newspapers*, edited by Claude E. Erbsen, 44–47. London: Innovation.

Fenton, Natalie, ed., 2010. *New Media, Old News: Journalism and Democracy in the Digital Age*. London: Sage.

Florini, Ann, ed., 2007. *The Right to Know, Transparency for an Open World*. New York: Columbia University Press.

Franklin, Bob, ed., 2011b. *The Future of Journalism*. London: Routledge.

Franklin, Bob, and Donica Mensing, eds., 2011. *Journalism Education, Training and Employment*. London: Routledge.

Fröhlich, Romy, and Christina Holtz-Bacha, eds., 2003. *Journalism Education in Europe and North America. An International Comparison*. Cresskill, NJ: Hampton Press.

Fuller, Jack. 1996. *News Values: Ideas for an Information Age*. Chicago: The University of Chicago Press.

Fuller, Jack. 2010. *What Is Happening to News? The Information Explosion and the Crisis in Journalism*. Chicago: The University of Chicago Press.

Gaunt, Philip. 1992. *Making the Newsmakers. International Handbook on Journalism Training*. Westport, CT: Greenwood Press.

Gillmor, Dan. 2004. *We the Media*. Sebastopol, CA: O'Reilly Media.

Gillmor, Dan. 2010. "Entrepreneurial Journalism". Paper presented at the World Journalism Education Congress, Grahamstown, South Africa, July 5–7. http://wjec.ru.ac.za.

Glasser, Theodore L. 2000. "The Politics of Public Journalism." *Journalism Studies* 1: 683–686.

Halman, Loek C. J. M., J. P. Sieben Inge, and Marga van Zundert. 2011. *The Atlas of European Values. Trends and Traditions at the Turn of the Century*. Leiden: Brill.

Hanitzsch, Thomas, Martin Löffelholz, and David H. Weaver. 2005. "Building a Home for the Study of Journalism." *Journalism* 6: 107–115.

Heikkilä, Heikki, Risto Kunelius, and Laura Ahva. 2011. "From Credibility to Relevance: Towards a Sociology of Journalism's 'Added Value'." In *The Future of Journalism*, edited by Bob Franklin, 190–200. London: Routledge.

Heinonen, Ari. 2011. "The Journalist's Relationship with Users: New Dimensions to Conventional Roles." In *Participatory Journalism. Guarding Open Gates at Online Newspapers*, edited by Jane B. Singer, Alfred Hermida, David Domingo, Ari Heinonen, Steve Paulussen, Thorsten Quandt, Zvi Reich and Marina Vujnovic, 34–55. Boston: Wiley-Blackwell.

Hermans, Liesbeth, and Maurice Vergeer. 2011. "Dutch Journalism in the New Millennium: Today's Occupational Role Conceptions Related to Journalistic Values and Background Characteristics." Paper presented at the ICA Conference, Boston, May.

Huibers, Theo.. 2008. *De uitgever aan het woord*. Delft: Thieme Grafi Media.

Hunter, Mark L., and Luk N. Van Wassenhove. 2010. *Disruptive News Technologies: Stakeholder Media and the Future of Watchdog Journalism Business Models*. Faculty and Research Working Paper. Fontainebleau: INSEAD.

Jarvis, Jeff. 2010. "Entrepreneurial Journalism." Keynote speech. http://www.fondspascaldecroos.org/inhoud/video/jeff-jarvis-journalists-entrepreneurs-keynote.

Josephi, Beate. 2009. "Journalism Education." In *The Handbook of Journalism Studies*, edited by Karin Wahl-Jorgensen and Thomas Hanitzsch, 42–56. London: Routledge.

Karlsson, Michael. 2011. "Rituals of Transparency: Evaluating Online News Outlets' Uses of Transparency in the United States, United Kingdom and Sweden." In *The Future of Journalism*, edited by Bob Franklin, 100–110. London: Routledge.

Kovach, Bill, and Tom Rosenstiel. 2001. *The Elements of Journalism*. New York: Crown Publishers.

Kramer, Mark. 2009. "On Narrative Journalism." http://www.vvoj.nl/cms/bio/mark-kramer/.

Küng, Lucy, Robert G. Picard, and Ruth Towse. 2008. *The Internet and the Mass Media*. London: Sage.

Lee-Wright, Peter, Angela Philips, and Tamara Witschge, eds., 2012. *Changing Journalism*. London: Routledge.

Luyendijk, Joris. 2009. "Naar een nieuwe journalistiek." Paper presented at Johan de Witt-lecture, Dordrecht, October.

Mensing, Donica. 2011. "Rethinking (Again) the Future of Journalism Education." In *The Future of Journalism*, edited by Bob Franklin. London: Routledge.

Mensing, Donica, and Bob Franklin. 2011. "Introduction. Journalism Education, Training and Employment." In *Journalism Education, Training and Employment*, edited by Bob Franklin and Donica Mensing, 1–10. London: Routledge.

Nip, Joyce. 2006. "Exploring the Second Phase of Public Journalism." *Journalism Studies* 7 (2): 212–236.

OECD Working Party on the Information Economy. 2007. "Participative Web: User-created Content." www.oecd.org/dataoecd/57/14/38393115.pdf.

Opgenhaffen, Michaël, Leen d'Haenens, and Maarten Corten. 2011. "Journalistiek in Vlaanderen: Afstemming tussen praktijk, opleiding en onderzoek." *Tijdschrift voor Communicatiewetenschap* 39 (3): 65–89.

Phillips, Angela. 2012. "Transparency and the Ethics of New Journalism." In *Changing Journalism*, edited by Peter Lee-Wright, Angela Philips and Tamara Witschge, 135–148. London: Routledge.

Rosen, Jay. 1999. "Interview. Nico Drok and Thijs Jansen. 1999. CDV in gesprek over civiele journalistiek. Interview met Jay Rosen." *Christen Democratische Verkenningen* 10: 3–13.

Rosen, Jay. 2008. "The People Formerly Known As Audience." In *Participation and Media Production. Critical Reflections on Content Creation*, edited by N. Carpentier and B. De Cleen, 163–165. Newcastle, UK: Cambridge Scholars.

Rosenberry, Jack, and Burton St.? John III. 2010. *Public Journalism 2.0: The Promise of a Citizen-engaged Press*. New York: Routledge.

Schröder, Kim C., and Bent S. Larsen. 2009 "The Shifting Cross-media News Landscape; Challenges for Journalism Practice." Paper presented at The Future of Journalism Conference, Cardiff University, September.

Splichal, Slavko, and Colin Sparks. 1994. *Journalists for the 21st Century*. Norwood, NJ: Ablex Publishing.

Singer, Jane B., Alfred Hermida, David Domingo, Ari Heinonen, Steve Paulussen, Thorsten Quandt, Zvi Reich, and Marina Vujnovic. 2011. *Participatory Journalism. Guarding Open Gates at Online Newspapers*. Boston: Wiley-Blackwell.

Terzis, Georgios, ed., 2009. *European Journalism Education*. Bristol, UK: Intellect.

Weaver, David H., Randal A. Beam, Bonnie J. Brownlee, Paul S. Voakes, and Cleveland G. Wilhoit. 2007. *The American Journalist in the 21st Century: U.S. News People at the Dawn of a New Millennium*. Mahwah, NJ: Lawrence Erlbaum.

Witschge, Tamara. 2012. "Changing Audiences, Changing Journalism?" In *Changing Journalism*, edited by Peter Lee-Wright, Angela Philips and Tamara Witschge, 99–114. London: Routledge.

Appendix A

Factor Analysis (Professionals)

	F1	F2	F3	F4	F5	F6	F7	F8	
	Personal	Analytical	Technical	Societal	Account	Genre	Civic	Narrative	Communality
9.3 Show initiative	**0.705**								0.565
8.3 Be willing to take criticism	**0.680**								0.603
9.5 Show insight in relations within a team	**0.668**								0.662
9.4 Show insight in own strengths and weaknesses	**0.666**				0.309				0.671
9.1 Have good social skills	**0.499**							0.369	0.557
5.3 Be able to interpret the selected information		**0.717**							0.643
5.1 Be able to distinguish between main and side issues		**0.711**							0.594
5.2 Be able to select information on the basis of reliability		**0.629**							0.593
4.1 Have a good general knowledge	0.382	**0.603**							0.544
4.3 Be able to use all required sources effectively		**0.534**							0.484
7.2 Present information in combinations of words, sounds and images			**0.727**						0.615
6.5 Be able use new media structuring techniques			**0.727**						0.589
7.4 Be able to work with technical infrastructure			**0.716**						0.631
1.1 Have a commitment to society				**0.781**					0.707
1.2 Have insight in the influence of journalism in society				**0.684**					0.636
1.4 Understand the values that underlie professional choices				**0.537**	0.336				0.521
8.2 Be able to evaluate own work	0.360				**0.627**				0.584
8.4 Be able to take responsibility for the choices made during the process		0.361			**0.603**				0.628
8.5 Be able to take responsibility for the product		0.399			**0.586**				0.571
5.4 Be able to select information in accordance with the genre						**0.822**			0.758
6.3 Be able to structure in accordance with the genre						**0.708**			0.640
6.2 Be able to fine-tune content and form					0.346	**0.478**		0.354	0.510
2.4 Be able to stimulate debate							**0.756**		0.690
4.5 Have the will to interact with the public			0.335				**0.637**		0.697
3.4 Be able to organize contributions from the public			0.458				**0.483**		0.542
6.1 Be able to use different types of narrative structures								**0.738**	0.620
10.1 Be able to present ideas convincingly					0.413		0.434	**0.527**	0.704
Eigenvalue	6.998	2.279	1.665	1.488	1.347	1.302	1.055	1.018	
Explained variance (%)	24.992	8.138	5.945	5.315	4.812	4.649	3.767	3.635	

Principal Component Analysis, Varimax with Kaiser-Normalization, nine iterations, total variance explained = 61.523 per cent; factor loadings <0.300 are not reported. Bold numbers represent highest factor loadings.

THE GLOBAL JOURNALIST IN THE TWENTY-FIRST CENTURY
A cross-national study of journalistic competencies

Lars Willnat, David H. Weaver, and **Jihyang Choi**

This study presents selected findings related to journalistic competencies or skills from surveys of more than 29,000 journalists working in 31 countries or territories, conducted between 1996 and 2011. The data come from survey studies included in Weaver and Willnat's 2012 book, The Global Journalist in the 21st Century. *The study focuses on aspects such as journalists' age and education, working conditions, professional values or orientations, opinions about the importance of different aspects of the job, and attitudes toward new reporting skills that are necessary to cope with a multimedia news environment. The study concludes that there are no clear patterns of such competency among the journalists included in this analysis. However, tendencies were observed for some countries to have younger, less experienced, less formally educated journalists who do not highly value the interpretive or analytical role of journalism, who are less satisfied with their work, who have less freedom in their work, and who lack the multimedia skills necessary in the age of online journalism. The study also calls for systematic content analysis studies that investigate whether self-reported competencies of journalists in each nation actually correlate with the quality of the news products they create.*

Introduction

Comparing journalists across national borders and cultures has become more complicated due to the dramatic changes in journalism during the past decade. In addition to the many individual, social, cultural, and political differences that might influence the work of journalists around the world, there has been a blurring of the boundaries between journalism and other forms of public communication, and between journalists and those formerly known as media audiences. In addition, the digital revolution that has led to a converged media environment has also had an impact on what skills or competencies today's journalist must possess to function effectively within modern media organizations (Cremedas and Lysak 2011; Deuze 2007).

These developments make it even more difficult to look for general patterns and trends in journalistic competencies—but not impossible. While some scholars have pointed out that even in Western societies substantial gaps exist in the desirable competencies and societal roles of journalists (Cokley et al. 2011), there are still some similarities that seem to cut across the boundaries of geography, culture, language, society, religion, race, and ethnicity.

The present study compares the professional competencies of news people in various diverse political and cultural environments. While the definition of journalistic competency itself is highly fluid, the aim of these comparisons is to try to identify some cross-national patterns of journalistic competencies or skills, assuming that these have some relationship to what is reported (and how it is covered) in the various news media around the world, and that this news coverage matters in terms of world public opinion and policies. We are also interested in whether there are any emerging global patterns of journalistic competencies that can be identified.

Method

This article presents selected findings related to journalistic competencies or skills from surveys conducted between 1996 and 2011 on more than 29,000 journalists working in 31 countries or territories. The data we analyze here come from a total of 42 survey studies included in the book *The Global Journalist in the 21st Century* (Weaver and Willnat 2012). These surveys were conducted in Australia, Belgium, Brazil, Great Britain, Canada, Chile, China, Colombia, Denmark, Finland, France, Germany, Hong Kong, Hungary, Indonesia, Israel, Japan, South Korea, Malaysia, the Netherlands, New Zealand, Poland, Russia, Singapore, Slovenia, Spain, Sweden, Switzerland, Taiwan, the United Arab Emirates, and the United States. In several countries, more than one survey was conducted (Columbia, Hong Kong, Indonesia, Israel, Switzerland, and the United States).[1]

These are representative surveys of journalists for the most part, but there are a few exceptions in cases where survey data on journalists was available for the first time (e.g., Malaysia and Indonesia). The response rates vary from a reported low of 12 percent in New Zealand to a reported high of 99 percent among Chinese journalists. Six of the 42 surveys were conducted by mail; three by mail and online means; one by mail, telephone and online means; eight by telephone; one by telephone and mail; two by telephone and online means; six were self-administered; one was both self-administered and online; six were based on personal (face-to-face) interviews; seven took place solely online, and one used all methods (see Table 1).

Although most of these surveys were conducted independently in the various societies represented here, the task of comparing the findings was made easier by the fact that many had borrowed questions from the questionnaires used in the American Journalist studies (Weaver and Wilhoit 1986, 1996; Weaver et al. 2007). Some of the surveys employed their own questions or modified the original wordings somewhat. Nevertheless, the thousands of interviews of journalists from these many countries constitute a solid data foundation for cross-national comparison purposes, keeping in mind the admonition of Blumler, McLeod, and Rosengren (1992) and Hallin and Mancini (2004) that things compared should be comparable.

The things about journalists that we compare in this article include those that we think are related to journalistic competencies or skills, including basic characteristics such as age, education levels and the proportions studying journalism in college. The working conditions compared include perceptions of amount of autonomy or freedom and job satisfaction (including predictors of this in a few societies). Professional values or orientations related to competency include the importance of different journalistic roles (such as reporting the news quickly, providing analysis and interpretation, investigating

TABLE 1
Sample sizes, dates, and methods of journalist surveys

	Sample size	Response rate (%)	Year of study	Representative survey[a]	Method(s) used
Asia					
China	1309	99.0	2010/11	Yes	Personal interviews
Hong Kong	553	62.0	1996	Yes	Self-administered
	722	62.0	2001	Yes	Self-administered
	1004	55.0	2006	Yes	Self-administered
Indonesia	385	80.0	2001/02	No	Personal interviews
	100	–	2007/08	No	Personal interviews
Japan	1011	18.4	2007	Yes	Mail
Korea	970	–	2009	Yes	Personal interviews
Malaysia	182	72.8	2009/10	No	Self-administered
Singapore	447	39.5	2009	No	Self-administered
Taiwan	1182	72.0	2004	Yes	Personal interviews
Australia/Pacific					
Australia	117	–	2009/10	No	Phone
New Zealand	514	12.0	2007	Yes	Online
Europe					
Belgium	682	30.6	2007/08	Yes	Mail and online
Denmark	2008	44.3	2009	Yes	Online
Finland	614	41.0	2007	Yes	Mail and online
France	405	87.0	2007	Yes	Phone
Germany	1536	72.8	2005	Yes	Phone and mail
Great Britain	1238	11.5	2001	Yes	Mail and online
Hungary	940	–	2006	Yes	Personal interviews
Netherlands	642	32.0	2006	Yes[a]	Mail
Poland	329	–	2009	Yes	Phone
Russia	796	–	2008	Yes	All methods
Slovenia	406	29.0	2009	Yes	Online
Spain	1000	–	2009	Yes	Phone
Sweden	621	52.0	2009	Yes[a]	Mail
Switzerland	2020	37.1	1998	Yes[a]	Mail
	449	38.8	2006/07	Yes	Online
	657	35.6	2007	Yes	Online
	1403	19.0	2008	Yes[a]	Mail
North America					
Canada	385	21.6	2007	Yes[a]	Mail
United States	1149	79.0	2002	Yes	Phone
	400	67.0	2007	Yes	Phone
South America					
Brazil	506	36.5	2009	Yes	Online
Chile	570	29.0	2009	Yes	Online
Colombia	300	–	2006	No	Phone and online
	217	–	2008	No	Phone and online
Middle East					
Arab journalists	601	–	2005/06	No	Self-administered and online
Israel	209	53.7	2002	Yes[a]	Phone and mail
	200	73.8	2004	Yes[a]	Phone
	333	47.4	2008	Yes	Phone
UAE	160	32.0	2000	No	Personal interviews and mail
Total *N*	29,272				

[a]Based on limited membership lists.

claims of government, etc.), opinions about the importance of different aspects of the job (pay, autonomy, public service, etc.), and attitudes toward new reporting skills that are necessary to cope with a media environment that often requires journalists to work across various media platforms.

Obviously, this approach is much more inductive than deductive. After all, we are comparing the aggregate findings of surveys that have been conducted during the past decade with a variety of methods and measures. However, the primary goal of this article is not to elaborate or test theories, but rather to discover cross-national patterns of similarities and differences that can provide a foundation of empirical data for future theorizing about journalistic competencies.

Demographic Characteristics

While age and education are not direct indicators of journalistic skills, they can reflect a journalist's work experience and competency. Older journalists tend to be more experienced in their jobs and hold more advanced job titles within their news organization. At the same time, though, it would be dangerous to conclude that journalists with a college degree are generally more skilled than their colleagues without such degrees. Because advanced journalism skills are often acquired on the job rather than in classrooms, any correlation that might exist between tertiary education and journalistic skills might be misleading.

Nevertheless, it seems important to document how educated journalists are, and how many of them hold advanced degrees in journalism in particular. We think that a larger number of media workers with a formal degree in journalism might indicate a trend toward greater professionalism in this occupation around the world.

As our survey studies indicate, journalism tends to be a young person's occupation in most nations. In most places, journalists are younger on average than is the work force in general. In many countries, young people become journalists to gain some experience before leaving for more lucrative and stable jobs in other fields, especially public relations. This seems to be a fairly common pattern around the world.

The average age of journalists ranges from 32 to 53 in the 29 surveys reporting it, with the youngest journalists coming from Australia, Britain, Chile, China, Hong Kong, Indonesia, Malaysia, Poland, Singapore, Taiwan, and the United Arab Emirates (UAE), where the average age is from 33 to 36, and the oldest from Denmark and Japan, where it is 45 and 53, respectively. Overall, this indicates that journalists from most countries do not stay too long in their jobs and therefore tend to have limited job experience.

This seems to be especially true for journalists from Asia. In China (39 percent), Hong Kong (36 percent), and Singapore (40 percent), for example, about 4 in 10 journalists have less than five years of work experience. Journalists in some European nations, on the other hand, can look back at significantly more work experience that often can be measured in decades rather than years. For example, the average journalist in Belgium (15 years), Denmark (17 years), and Finland (16 years) has spent more than one and a half decades on the job.

Although most journalists hold a four-year college degree, this is not the case in several countries, as Table 2 indicates. The locations with the lowest proportions of college graduate journalists are Finland, Germany, Hong Kong, Israel, New Zealand, Slovenia, and

TABLE 2
Basic demographic characteristics

	Average age	Hold a college degree (%)	Majored in journalism (%)
Australia	35.0[a]	80.0	35.0
Belgium	42.0	90.4	58.0
Brazil	39.8	100.0	100.0
Canada	–	78.7	–
Chile	35.6	92.5	86.2
China	33.1	93.4	–
Colombia	41.8	–	–
Denmark	45.0	88.0	70.0
Finland	–	38.0	25.0
France	42.2	–	14.8[c]
Germany	41.0	69.0	31.0[d]
Great Britain	34.0	–	–
Hong Kong	32.0[b]	71.7	56.8
Hungary	39.0	83.0	32.0
Indonesia	35.0	87.8	53.5
Israel	38.6	70.8	23.9
Japan	53.3	95.6	15.0
Malaysia	35.0	91.2	30.4
Netherlands	44.0	82.0	43.0[c]
New Zealand	39.0[a]	68.0	–
Poland	34.0[a]	84.2	31.6
Russia	41.0	90.0	44.1
Singapore	35.0	88.9	–
Slovenia	40.0	66.0	57.0
South Korea	38.6	97.1	21.9
Spain	43.0	93.9	74.8
Sweden	44.5	78.0	46.0
Switzerland	43.0	56.0	21.4
Taiwan	35.9	96.5	29.5
UAE	36.0	78.7	26.9
United States	41.0[a]	89.0	36.0
Overall means	39.2	82.1	42.5

[a]Median reported instead of mean.
[b]Estimate based on age groups.
[c]Includes professional school degrees.
[d]Includes journalism and media studies.

Switzerland—all below three-fourths. Those with the highest are Brazil, Japan, South Korea, and Taiwan—all above 95 percent. Only one country (Finland) reports less than half of its journalists holding a college degree. The average for all 28 countries reporting this figure is 82 percent, so it is far more common than not for journalists to be college graduates in this group, although the variation across countries is substantial.

It is less typical for journalists to be graduates of college journalism programs, however. Of the 25 nations reporting this figure, the average is 42.5 percent. Only eight countries reported more than half of their journalists had concentrated on journalism in college. In the other 17 countries or territories reporting this proportion, most did not exceed one-third, with the lowest figures from Finland, France, Israel, Japan, South Korea, and Switzerland. Thus, whatever journalistic benefits or deficiencies can be attributed to journalism education must be tempered by the fact that most journalists are not graduates of college-level journalism programs in this sample of nations.

Overall, it is fair to conclude that journalists in most nations are fairly young and highly educated, although significant differences exist. This seems to be especially true for the "concentrated on journalism in college" figure. Journalists with a journalism degree are still the exception in most nations, a finding that has not changed considerably during the past 20 years (Weaver 1998). A trend toward greater professionalism in journalism around the world as a result of more graduates coming out of college-level journalism programs therefore is not very likely.

Job Satisfaction and Perceived Autonomy

During the last two decades, the work environment of journalists around the world has been transformed dramatically. News-media ownership became more consolidated when a severe recession led to staff reductions and layoffs. Potential threats to professional autonomy emerged as news organizations became more market-driven and "civic journalism" challenged the traditional relationship among journalists, sources, and audience members.

Many of these changes can be traced to the influence of the internet on journalistic work and news organizations that have embraced online media to reach additional audiences with more targeted and frequently updated news. However, the specific demands of online news have also changed the way modern journalists work. While the internet and social media made it easier for journalists to research and report their stories, many of them are now expected to write a story, shoot still pictures or video, and then edit their own work for multiple media platforms. These are new professional obligations that might increase the risk of burnout, exhaustion, and stress among journalists (Deprez and Raeymaeckers 2012).

Given these significant changes in modern news organizations, it seems important to ask how these developments have influenced the work environment of journalists. Obviously the working conditions of journalists differ widely in the nations represented in this study, not only in terms of material resources but also in professional autonomy, political pressures, and journalistic norms and traditions that affect the subjects and approaches taken in reporting the news of the day. However, there are also common attitudes and perceptions that are shared by journalists across nations, which therefore can be analyzed from a comparative perspective.

The present analysis focuses on job satisfaction as one of the most important indicators of the working conditions of journalists, which in some cases is linked to their perceived autonomy or freedom. In the United States, for example, declining levels of job satisfaction and perceived autonomy have gone hand-in-hand since the early 1970s (Weaver et al. 2007). Job satisfaction also is an important indicator of journalistic competency because it "creates confidence, loyalty and ultimately improved quality in the output of the employed" (Tietjen and Myers 1998, 226). A recent survey study by Deprez and Raeymaeckers (2012), for example, found that Flemish journalists with higher levels of job satisfaction tend to value journalistic creativity, variation in media content, professional contacts, and intellectual challenges in their work. In addition, our own analysis of the survey data included in *The Global Journalist in the 21st Century* (Weaver and Willnat 2012) shows that journalists' rating of how well their news organization is informing the public is the best predictor of job satisfaction in Japan, Singapore, and the United States, and the second strongest predictor in Taiwan. Other predictors of job satisfaction across nations include ability to serve society, ability to cover a subject, and ability to help people—all of which could be considered indicators of journalistic quality or competency. We therefore feel confident to use job satisfaction as an indicator of journalistic competency in countries with different journalistic traditions.

Job satisfaction has been studied among journalists from many nations (Barrett 1984; Deprez and Raeymaeckers 2012; Man Chan, Pan, and Lee 2004; Powers 1991; Pollard 1995; Reinardy 2007; Stamm and Underwood 1993; Weaver and Wilhoit 1986, 1996; Weaver et al. 2007). Most of these studies agree that various factors can influence a journalist's job satisfaction, including organizational characteristics, assessments of organizational goals, priorities or conditions, and individual characteristics of journalists (Weaver et al. 2007). A recent analysis of job satisfaction among American journalists, for example, found that those journalists who perceived that they had substantial autonomy to decide which stories to work on and what to emphasize in their stories were happier, as were journalists who perceived themselves as having greater influence within the newsroom (Weaver et al. 2007).

The following analyses are based on surveys from 18 nations that included questions on journalists' job satisfaction and perceived job autonomy. While both of these concepts have been recognized as important variables in research on journalists, the survey questions that have been used to measure these two concepts differ slightly from study to study. As a result, the reported levels of job satisfaction and perceived job autonomy might be somewhat affected by question wording. However, the underlying meaning of these measurements is close enough to be compared across nations.

Job Satisfaction

The proportions of journalists considering themselves "very satisfied" with their jobs varies greatly among the nations that reported this, as Figure 1 indicates. Those countries or territories with the smallest percentages of very satisfied journalists were Chile, Hong Kong, South Korea, Taiwan, and the UAE, with Singapore and Slovenia not far behind; those with the largest were Colombia, Finland, and Israel. Some countries with relatively high percentages—such as Colombia, Finland, and Israel—reported relatively high figures for perceived autonomy as well.[2]

The average for all 18 countries that reported "very" satisfied figures was 25.7 percent. Overall, this indicates fairly low job satisfaction levels among journalists from most of the nations analyzed here. Even in nations with strong journalistic traditions such as Australia (38 percent), Canada (30 percent), Sweden (29 percent), and the United States (33 percent), only about a third of all journalists reported that they were very satisfied with their jobs.

Perceived Job Autonomy

The journalists with the highest perceived job autonomy were from Australia, Canada, and Finland, where more than three-fourths claimed to have a great deal of freedom on the job, as Figure 1 shows. Those countries with the fewest journalists claiming a great deal of freedom were Chile, Hong Kong, South Korea, and Taiwan. The

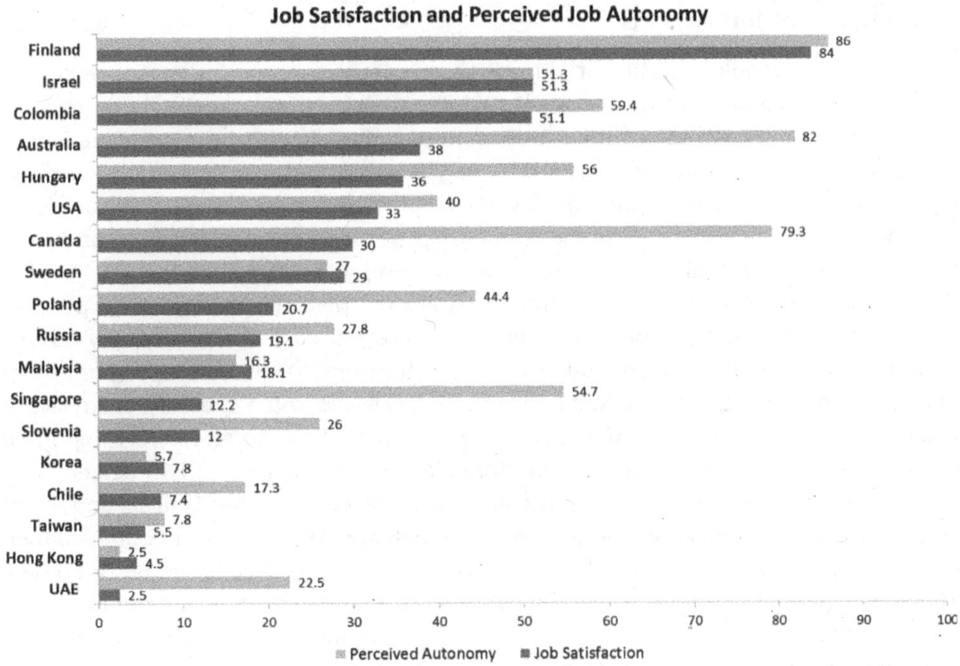

FIGURE 1
Job satisfaction and perceived job autonomy (% saying "very satisfied")

average for all 18 countries that reported "very satisfied" figures for perceived job autonomy was 39.2 percent. Overall, this indicates that in most nations only a minority of journalists perceive high levels of job autonomy.[3]

Perceived Job Autonomy and Job Satisfaction

Figure 1 also shows that the proportions of journalists perceiving a great deal of freedom are correlated ($r = 0.78$, $p < 0.001$) with the proportions claiming to be very satisfied with their jobs in several countries or territories, including Colombia, Finland, Israel, and the United States. This is not the case in Australia, Canada, and Singapore, however, where high percentages for perceived freedom were associated with low proportions of those who claimed to be very satisfied. These findings suggest that other factors besides perceived freedom contributed to job satisfaction in these countries.

Independent analyses of the survey data in some of the nations included in this study confirm this assumption. In Australia, for example, editorial policy was a stronger predictor of job satisfaction than perceived autonomy. Other predictors seemed to play a role, especially among the least satisfied journalists. In Chile, the strongest predictors of job satisfaction (or lack of it) were pay and the chance for journalists to use all of their abilities and knowledge. In Japan, the best predictors were the journalists' evaluations of the practices of their news organizations and their relationships with the government. In only four countries was perceived freedom on the job ranked as the most important predictor of job satisfaction—Finland, South Korea, Poland, and Russia.

Important Job Aspects

Another possible indicator of journalistic competence is which dimensions of their jobs journalists consider most important. We hypothesize that journalists who consider certain professional aspects of their jobs important are likely to be more experienced, competent, and skilled. In this part of the analysis we look at how important journalists from 14 nations consider editorial policy, developing a specialty, and job autonomy in their daily work. We also examine the relationship between the perceived importance of job autonomy and actual job autonomy, as indicated by these journalists.

Table 3 shows that journalists from Australia (67 percent), Indonesia (73 percent), and the United States (69 percent) were most likely to rate editorial policy as very important, whereas those least likely to do so were from Germany (21 percent), South Korea (19.5 percent), and Russia (22 percent). As for developing a specialty, journalists in Poland (79 percent) and the UAE (72 percent) were most likely to rate it very important, whereas those least likely to do so were from Slovenia and Spain (both 16 percent).

Even on perceived freedom on the job, a journalistic norm that Splichal and Sparks (1994) identified as similar among journalism students from 22 different countries, there were notable differences among the journalists interviewed in the studies reported here. Those from Poland (86 percent) were most likely to say that freedom on the job is very important, followed by those in Australia (64 percent) and Slovenia (63 percent), while those least likely to say so were from Spain (25 percent), Russia (28 percent), and South Korea (29 percent). Overall, there does seem to be more agreement on the importance of this journalistic norm than on others, as Splichal and Sparks (1994) argue, but there is still considerable variance between countries.

Importance of Job Autonomy and Perceived Job Autonomy

A comparison of how important journalists think job autonomy[4] is and how much job autonomy they actually perceive in their job shows only a moderate relationship

TABLE 3
Important job aspects

	Percentage saying "very important"		
	Editorial policy	**Developing a specialty**	**Job autonomy**
Australia	67.0	50.0	64.0
Chile	39.1	34.2	48.2
Colombia	–	–	59.4
Germany	21.0	–	42.0
Indonesia	73.1	62.1	61.6
Malaysia	58.1	53.3	33.9
Poland	56.2	79.0	85.7
Russia	21.8	19.2	27.8
Singapore	45.9	44.9	43.1
Slovenia	–	16.0	63.0
South Korea	19.5	27.2	28.9
Spain	–	16.2	24.8
UAE	61.9	71.9	53.8
United States	69.2	40.5	56.4
Overall means	48.4	42.9	49.5

($r = 0.46$, $p = 0.12$). As Figure 2 shows, in Poland, Slovenia, Indonesia, the United States, and the UAE, a majority of journalists rank the importance of job autonomy very highly, but, at the same time, also perceive relatively low levels of actual freedom in their jobs.

The largest gaps between the stated importance of job autonomy and perceived actual job autonomy are found in Poland (−41.3 percent), Indonesia (−37.4 percent), and Slovenia (−37.0 percent). Thus, it is clear that journalists from these nations perceive a large gap between what they do and what they think they should do. The one exception is Colombia, where a slight majority of journalists think that job autonomy is very important but also perceive relatively high levels of freedom in their jobs.

In other nations, such as Chile, Malaysia, and South Korea, less than half of the journalists think that job autonomy is very important, but also acknowledge that actual job autonomy is low. Less than a third of the journalists in Russia believe that job autonomy is a very important aspect in their work. At the same time, though, only about a third of the Russian journalists think that actual job autonomy is very high.

Overall, these patterns indicate that most journalists around the world recognize the importance of job autonomy, but also perceive large gaps between the ideal of autonomy and the actual freedoms they have. However, these gaps in perception are not restricted to nations with limited press freedom. Journalists from the United States, for example, perceive a substantial gap between their actual independence on the job and how much they value job autonomy as a journalistic ideal—despite the fact that they operate in a relatively free journalistic environment.

How are these findings related to journalistic competency? We think that gaps between perceived importance of autonomy and perceived actual freedom signal

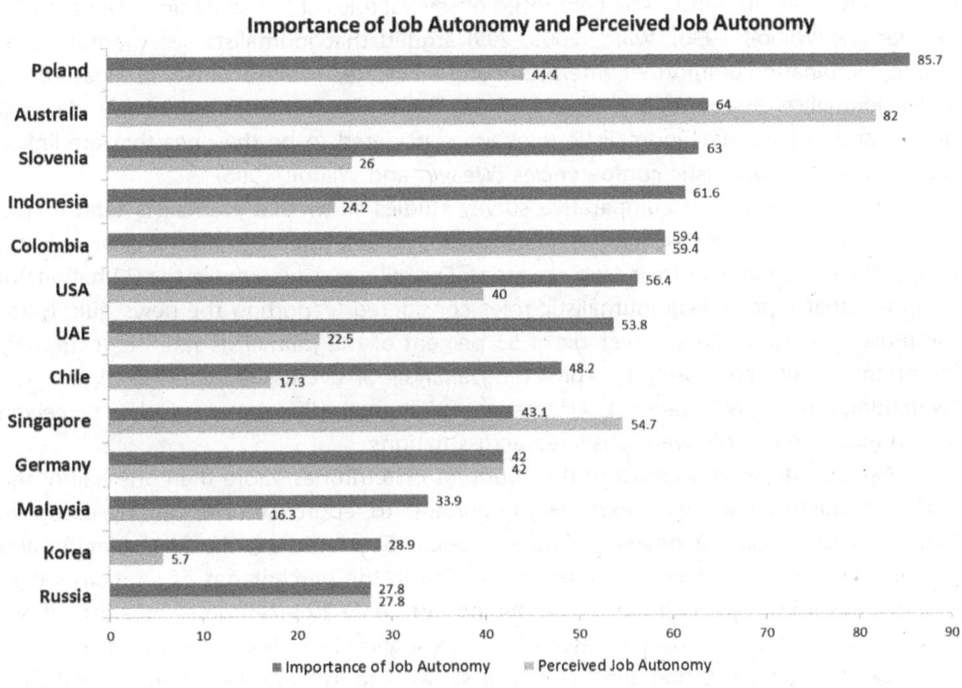

FIGURE 2
Importance of job autonomy and perceived job autonomy (% saying "very important" for job autonomy and % saying "very satisfied" for perceived job autonomy)

restrictions on what journalists are able to do in their work. They may have the skills and values necessary for high-quality journalism, but perceive limitations in their freedom to do their work as they think it should be done.

We hypothesize that journalists who do not think that the more professional aspects of their work are very important are less likely to be considered competent or professional by other journalists or their audiences. However, we realize that perceived importance of job aspects is not a direct measure of journalistic competency or skill, but rather a more direct measure of journalistic professionalism, which we think is positively correlated with journalistic competency.

Professional Roles

How journalists define their desired roles in society is closely related to the professional competencies of journalists. This is because their perceived roles tend to set the boundaries of journalistic skills, knowledge, and abilities. However, it is debatable whether all journalists share common professional roles, because the knowledge on which their journalistic practices are based is "both limited and less clearly defined" compared to other classical professions (Tumber and Prentoulis 2005, 58). Some of these debates have focused on whether journalism is a true profession (Beam 1990; Lawrence 1903; Splichal and Sparks 1994; Weaver and Wilhoit 1986), and some on whether journalism should even be called one (Bowman 1996; Glasser 1992).

Previous studies have shown that journalists' perceptions of their own roles are not one-dimensional, but tend to be composed of several roles at the same time (Deuze 2002; Weaver and Wilhoit 1996). Ward (2009, 299) argued that journalists see themselves as "some combination of informer, interpreter and advocate." While a variety of measures by which journalists assess their profession exist in the literature, "interpretive," "disseminator," and "adversarial" journalistic roles are considered to be the ones that are linked most closely to journalistic competencies (Weaver and Wilhoit 1996).

The findings of our comparative survey studies show that journalists tend to put more emphasis on one role than on another, depending upon the institutional, cultural, and political situations in their own countries. Overall, news workers in the 22 nations or territories that reported on journalistic roles considered "reporting the news quickly" as the most important role (an average of 53 percent of the journalists rated it "extremely important"), followed closely by "providing analysis of events" (49.2 percent), and the "watchdog" role (39.2 percent). However, substantial differences in the perceived importance of each role were observed across nations.

As Table 4 shows, in most of the countries or territories, more than one-half of the journalists agreed that it was "extremely important" to report the news quickly, except in Brazil, Canada, Chile, Denmark, Germany, Japan, South Korea, the Netherlands, and Taiwan. Nevertheless, there was notable variation in the percentages of journalists who thought this role was very important—ranging from only 2 percent in Denmark to about 88 percent in the UAE. Possible reasons for this variation include competition from other news media, the type of medium the journalists worked for, and the potentially different norms and values of journalists from these countries.

Considerable differences also were found for the perception of the analytical function of news media, or "providing analysis of complex problems." Among

TABLE 4
Professional roles

	Percentage saying "extremely important"		
	Report news quickly	**Provide analysis of events**	**Be watchdog of government**
Australia	80.0	72.0	90.0
Belgium	80.0	93.0	69.0
Brazil	38.0	72.2	14.6
Canada	37.9	51.7	45.2
Chile	40.7	–	38.9
Denmark	2.0	55.0	56.0
Germany	42.0	40.0	7.0
Hong Kong	51.0	36.2	23.3
Indonesia	–	9.0	39.0
Japan	33.5	6.2	2.5
Malaysia	78.3	62.2	21.0
Netherlands	33.0	37.0	18.0
Poland	81.7	65.4	42.6
Russia	80.5	77.8	53.0
Singapore	58.6	45.0	35.6
Slovenia	58.0	57.0	51.0
South Korea	17.5	23.4	40.0
Sweden	55.0	32.0	22.0
Switzerland	–	36.9	26.9
Taiwan	47.2	43.1	32.9
UAE	88.1	68.1	61.9
United States	59.0	51.0	71.0
Overall means	53.0	49.2	39.2

the 21 countries or territories where this role was measured, journalists in Japan (6.2 percent) and Indonesia (9 percent) were least likely to consider it very important. The countries where this role was most likely to be considered very important included Australia, Belgium, Brazil, Malaysia, Poland, Russia, and Sweden—a diverse mix of older and younger democracies.

The most noticeable variation in perceptions was found in the "watchdog" role. While the importance of such a role is acknowledged by journalists around the world, its exact meaning tends to be defined differently across countries and cultures. On investigating government claims (or being a watchdog of government) the range was as wide as it was for reporting news quickly (from 2.5 percent in Japan to 90 percent in Australia), with journalists most likely to consider this role very important coming from the more democratic countries of Belgium and the United States.

Those least likely to see this watchdog role as very important were from Brazil, Germany, and Japan, possibly because of the closer ties between journalists and government officials in these societies and an emphasis on different roles. Köcher (1986), for example, argued in her article that German journalists tend to be "missionaries" rather than "bloodhounds." In Japan, where only 2.5 percent supported the watchdog role of the media, there is little incentive for journalists to investigate government claims because of the *Kisha* (journalist) club system, which tightly controls access to news sources and press conferences (Cooper-Chen 1997; Feldman 1993; Takeshita and Ida 2009).

The type of media system is another influence on journalists' perception and understanding of the watchdog role. Malaysian journalists, for example, were less likely to support the traditional "watchdog" role (21 percent), which might be attributed to the constraints placed on them by the various laws and regulations that limit press freedom in Malaysia (Tamam, Raj, and Govindasamy 2012).

Overall then, there was more disagreement than agreement over the relative importance of these journalistic roles considered together, which is hardly evidence to support the universal occupational standards mentioned by Splichal and Sparks (1994). In fact, none of the three roles was considered to be very important by more than 53 percent of all journalists on average.

The reasons for this disagreement are difficult to specify for so many possible comparisons, but a secondary analysis of the data from journalists in China, Taiwan, and the United States by Zhu et al. (1997) suggests that political system similarities and differences are far more important than cultural similarities and differences, organizational constraints or individual characteristics in predicting the variance in how journalists perceive their roles.

The differences in journalists' views about which professional roles are more or less important also have implications for journalistic competencies. If, for example, journalists in a certain country value the neutral disseminator role, the skills needed to perform this role in that country will differ somewhat from those needed in another country where the interpretive or adversarial role is valued more highly.

Of course, there will be some overlap in skills needed to perform these roles well, but techniques of investigative reporting, for example, would be more necessary for the adversarial role than the neutral disseminator role. And we would expect that such techniques would be more likely to be taught in journalism schools and on the job in countries where a higher percentage of journalists value highly the adversarial or watchdog role. The same could be said for the skills of analysis in countries where higher percentages of journalists value the interpretive role. Whether this is actually true requires further research into the education of journalists in various countries, as well as content analyses comparing the kinds of news coverage that journalists produce in these different countries.

New Reporting Skills

In many societies, journalistic competencies have been related to several desirable journalistic roles, such as information disseminator, interpreter, or watchdog of government (Weaver 1998; Weaver and Wilhoit 1996). Specific reporting skills, such as investigative reporting techniques, have been developed among journalists around the world to fulfill these roles. However, journalists also are constantly pressured to redefine their roles and readjust their reporting skills in response to institutional, economic, and political changes and an evolving media environment.

The findings presented in our surveys of journalists suggest that several new reporting skills are required to adapt to the ongoing changes in newsgathering and news consumption, while an emphasis on traditional skills and practices remains.

One of the most pressing needs mentioned by journalists in various countries was the acquisition of new multimedia skills. As mentioned earlier, with digitalization and convergence reshaping newsrooms and news practices, more and more journalists need to be able to produce and process text, video, and sound in their reporting.

For example, 60 percent of British journalists noted as early as 2001 that new or additional skills were needed to improve their work in areas that deal with information technologies and new media. Seven years later, more than three-fourths of journalists in Belgium responded that online research skills (90 percent), multimedia skills (80 percent), and technological skills (77 percent) are 'very important for their reporting. Thus, multimedia skills have become an important aspect of journalistic competency (Deuze 2007).

Concerns about higher workloads and the pressure to acquire such new reporting skills were noted frequently. For example, 45 percent of Finnish journalists noted in 2007 that their daily work with multimedia has increased dramatically over time. However, while journalists recognize that they have to spend more time and energy to adapt to the new media environment, it seems that at least some think positively about these changes. Most French journalists, for instance, said in 2007 that multimedia journalism is more of a "benefit" (62 percent) than a "threat" (34 percent).

Another competency needed in the new media environment is interpretation skills. While interpretative reporting is not a new phenomenon, straight and factual reporting has long been the norm in journalism (Hallin 2000). However, due to the proliferation of online media and 24-hour news, and the subsequent flood of raw and unfiltered information, the dominant role of journalists in many countries is changing toward offering interpretation of the information reported on (Bardoel 1996; Tumber 2001). This shift in role is reflected in recent survey findings (2006–2009), which show that journalists from several countries (Belgium, Brazil, Canada, Denmark, the Netherlands, and Slovenia) now believe that interpretation is one of their most important roles—even more important than the dissemination of information in some cases.

Tumber and Prentoulis (2005) explain that two aspects of the new communication environment are promoting the importance of interpretative journalism: the increased number of news providers, and the tendency of owners of content rights to communicate directly with an audience, bypassing journalists and traditional media. Thus, given the abundance of raw information available to audiences, journalists will need to show their abilities in sorting out meaningful facts and interpreting them (Bardoel 1996; Tumber 2001; Tumber and Bromley 1998).

Another set of reporting skills that might have gained importance due to the demands of around-the-clock news are those that enable journalists to report the news quickly. As Deuze (2005, 449) noted, the work of modern journalists tends to have "an aura of instantaneity and immediatism" because it involves the "notions of speed, fast decision-making, haste, and working in accelerated real-time."

However, the success of new media and the changes it brought to journalism have led to mixed predictions about the importance of quick reporting. Some scholars have argued that speed of reporting will become more important in a 24/7 digital environment (Hall 2001; Pavlik 1999). Others argue that the growth of new communication technologies has depressed the importance of the disseminating function. Certainly, studies among US journalists suggest that this disseminator function is seen as less important than in the past (Weaver et al. 2007).

The fact that several countries in our study reported a decline in the importance of "reporting news quickly" during last few years might reflect journalists' rather ambivalent attitudes toward the continued importance of the news disseminator role. In the United States, for example, the majority of journalists (59 percent) still consider reporting the news quickly to be a "very important" role, but this percentage dropped 10 points between 1992 and 2002. In Canada, the importance of getting information to the public quickly dropped from second place in 1996 to sixth place in 2007. Similarly, in South Korea, the importance of getting information to the public dropped from fourth place in 1999 to eighth place in 2009.

Conclusions

Based on the findings of surveys conducted among journalists from 31 nations and territories, this article compared the professional competencies of news people in diverse political and cultural environments. Among the various dimensions that could represent journalistic competency, we focused on journalists' basic demographic characteristics, working conditions, professional values or orientations, opinions about the importance of different aspects of the job, and attitudes toward new reporting skills that are necessary to cope with a multimedia environment.

What have we learned from these cross-national comparisons? First, it is clear that journalism is dominated by relatively young professionals in most of the nations analyzed here. The average journalist in our study is 39 years old, but in many nations such as Australia, Great Britain, China, Hong Kong, Indonesia, Malaysia, Poland, and Singapore journalists tend to be much younger.

The relatively low average age of journalists is explained partly by the fact that they do not stay too long in their jobs and therefore tend to have limited job experience. This seems to be especially true for journalists from Asia. In China, Hong Kong, and Singapore, for example, almost 4 in 10 journalists have less than five years of work experience. Journalists in some European nations, on the other hand, can look back at significantly more work experience. This suggests that European journalists may be more competent than others.

As expected, journalists around the world tend to be highly educated. Overall, 8 in 10 journalists in our study held a college degree, although some regional differences were observed. The locations with the lowest proportions of college graduate journalists are Finland, Germany, Hong Kong, Israel, New Zealand, Slovenia, and Switzerland—all below three-fourths. Those with the highest are Brazil, Japan, South Korea, and Taiwan. On this measure, then, some European journalists might be judged to be less competent than some Asian journalists.

Despite the fact that most journalists in our study attended college, it is clear that many of them did not focus on journalism in their studies. Overall, less than half of the journalists in our samples are graduates of college-level journalism programs. Only eight countries reported more than half of their journalists had concentrated on journalism in college. In the other 17 countries or territories reporting this proportion, most did not exceed one-third, with the lowest figures coming from Finland, France, Israel, Japan, South Korea, and Switzerland.

Thus, journalistic competency might be higher in those nations where journalists are more likely to have studied journalism in college. Of course, such a conclusion might be challenged by those who argue that true journalistic competency can only be acquired on the job. In other words, journalists without a formal journalism education might be able to compensate for this lack in training with more years of actual job experience.

It is also important to note that there does not seem to be a trend toward more tertiary journalism education around the world. A comparison of our current findings with results from an earlier study by Weaver (1998) shows that the average percentage of journalists with a journalism degree increased only marginally from 41.5 percent in 1998 to 42.5 percent in 2012. It therefore appears that journalistic competencies are still acquired mostly on the job rather than at universities.

Finally, we would like to acknowledge that education and seniority (or age) among journalists could vary because of country-specific market conditions, government policies, or vocational requirements. However, the relative consistency of these two demographic variables among journalists from around the world coupled with the fact that age and education usually are good indicators of professional accomplishment, leaves us comfortable enough to conclude that they are important indicators of journalistic competency.

Another focus of this comparative analysis was job satisfaction. As we mentioned earlier, journalists' perceived happiness or gratification in their jobs can be considered an important indicator of journalistic competency because it might create confidence, loyalty, and improved quality in output (Tietjen and Myers 1998). Unfortunately, what we found is that only one in four journalists in the nations and territories analyzed here were very satisfied with their jobs.

Countries with the smallest percentages of very satisfied journalists were Chile, Hong Kong, South Korea, Taiwan, and the UAE; those with the largest were Colombia, Finland, and Israel. Even in nations with strong journalistic traditions such as Australia, Canada, Sweden, and the United States, only about a third of all journalists reported that they were very satisfied with their jobs.

This is a worrisome finding because it indicates that the vast majority of journalists around the world are not happy in their jobs and therefore likely to look for other employment possibilities—which, in turn, would negatively affect the average level of job experience. Moreover, it appears that journalists in many nations do not perceive much individual independence and freedom in their jobs.

At the same time, though, it appears that job satisfaction correlates with perceived job autonomy in many nations. Journalists in Colombia, Finland, and Israel, for example, reported high levels of job satisfaction and job autonomy, while media workers in South Korea, Taiwan, and Hong Kong claimed extremely low satisfaction and autonomy in their jobs. Since these correlations were found in most of the nations and territories analyzed here, it is fair to conclude that the independence and freedom journalists experience in their jobs usually corresponds with perceived levels of job satisfaction.

Despite the central role job autonomy plays in the daily work of journalists, a comparison of how important journalists think job autonomy is and how much job autonomy they actually perceive in their job shows a rather weak relationship. Overall, the patterns we observed indicate that many journalists are not only unhappy about how free they are in their work, but also perceive large gaps between the ideal of autonomy and the actual freedoms they have.

We believe that these gaps between perceived job autonomy and actual freedom signal restrictions on what journalists are able to do in their work. They may have the skills and values necessary for high-quality journalism, but clearly perceive limitations in their freedom to do their work as they think it should be done.

In addition to perceptions of job satisfaction and job autonomy, we also focused on ideas about journalistic roles. We argued that how journalists define their desired roles in society is closely related to their professional competencies because their roles tend to set the boundaries of journalistic skills, knowledge and abilities.

What we found, however, was far more disagreement than agreement over the relative importance of these journalistic roles. For example, only slightly more than half of the journalists agreed that it was important to report the news quickly, and agreement ranged from a low of 2 percent in Denmark to about 88 percent in the UAE.

Similarly, the role of "providing analysis of complex problems" found support among half of the interviewed journalists, but again ranged from a low of 6 percent in Japan to a high of 93 percent in Belgium. However, the most variation in perception was found in the "watchdog" role, which was supported by only about 4 in 10 journalists overall. While journalists in democratic countries were slightly more likely to support this classic journalistic role, support ranged from a low of 7 percent in Germany to 90 percent in Australia.

As we have argued earlier, these differences in journalists' views about which professional roles are more or less important also have implications for journalistic competencies. Journalists who value the neutral disseminator role, for example, will need to develop a set of skills that will differ somewhat from the skills needed to carry out the interpretive or adversarial role. Thus, professional competencies might depend on what specific journalistic roles a given media system favors or supports.

One of the most pressing needs mentioned by journalists in various countries was the acquisition of new multimedia skills. With digitalization and convergence reshaping newsrooms and news practices, journalists increasingly need to be able to produce and process text, video, and sound in their reporting. While the hiring of young journalists (who grew up with digital media and often received multimedia training at universities or trade schools) will somewhat alleviate the pressure to formally push for more digital skills in newsrooms around the world, it is also clear that some of the older journalists need to catch up.

Another competency needed in the new media environment is interpretation skills. While interpretative reporting is not a new phenomenon, the dominant role of journalists in many countries is slowly changing toward interpretation because of the growing flood of raw and unfiltered information available online. This shift in role is reflected in our findings, where journalists from several countries (Belgium, Brazil, Canada, Denmark, the Netherlands, and Slovenia) now believe that interpretation is one of their most important roles.

Other reporting skills that have gained importance due to the demands of around-the-clock news are those that enable journalists to report the news quickly. However, the fact that journalists in several countries reported a decline in the importance of "reporting news quickly" in the last few years reflects journalists' rather ambivalent attitudes toward the continued importance of the news disseminator role.

This decline in the perceived importance of reporting news quickly seems to contradict the growing trend toward 24/7 online journalism. Because we cannot be sure that this trend is indeed a global phenomenon, future research should investigate whether this important journalistic role indeed is losing ground among journalists who are undoubtedly under more pressure every day to create and publish news faster.

Overall then, it is clear from the data presented in this study, and the more detailed information contained in *The Global Journalist in the 21st Century* (Weaver and Willnat 2012), that journalistic competency is a complex concept that can be assessed in many different ways, and that there are no clear patterns of such competency in the countries and territories included in this book.

Nevertheless, we observed tendencies for some countries to have younger, less experienced, less formally educated journalists who do not highly value the interpretive/analytical role of journalism, who are less satisfied with their work, who have less freedom in their work, and who lack the multimedia skills necessary for online journalism. In such countries, it seems reasonable to assume that journalists are less competent than those in countries with the opposite characteristics. But such an assumption can only be verified with systematic content analyses that would investigate whether the self-reported competencies of journalists in each nation actually correlate with the quality of the news products they create.

ACKNOWLEDGEMENTS

The authors of this article would like to thank the following scholars for contributing national survey data to this comparative study: Erik Albæk, Jesus Arroyave, Marsha Barber, Marta Milena Barrios, Randal A. Beam, Marc-François Bernier, Peter Bro, Bonnie J. Brownlee, Heinz Bonfadelli, Joseph M. Chan, Mikhail Chernysh, Claes de Vreese, Pedro Farias, Mitsuru Fukuda, Cherian George, Jeremy Ginges, Manimaran Govindasamy, Mark Hanna, Thomas Hanitzsch, Xiaoming Hao, Ari Heinonen, Liesbeth Hermans, Heloiza Golbspan Herscovitz, Dedy N. Hidayat, James Hollings, Beate Josephi, Jyrki Jyrkiäinen, Guido Keel, Jeroen De Keyser, Sung Tae Kim, Mohamed Kirat, Peter Lah, Geoff Lealand, Francis L. F. Lee, Ven-hwei Lo, Maja Malik, Mirko Marr, Aralynn Abare McMane, Claudia Mellado, Oren Meyers, Lars Nord, Jakub Nowak, Shinji Oi, Szymon Ossowski, Svetlana Pasti, Steve Paulussen, Lawrence Pintak, Alexander Pleijter, Lidia Pokrzycka, Karin Raeymaeckers, Sony Jalarajan Raj, Ian Richards, Sergio Roses, Francisco Javier Paniagua Rojano, Shinsuke Sako, Karen Sanders, Armin Scholl, Adam Shehata, Morten Skovsgaard, Agnieszka Stepinska, Jesper Strömbäck, Luiza Svitich, Clement Y. K. So, Young Jun Son, Ezhar Tamam, Yariv Tsfati, Maria Vasarhelyi, Maurice Vergeer, Siegfried Weischenberg, Vinzenz Wyss, Hongzhong Zhang, and Suzana Žilič-Fišer.

NOTES

1. In Columbia, two surveys were conducted. In 2006, 300 journalists from the five main Colombian cities (Bogotá, Medellin, Cali, Barranquilla, and Cartagena) were interviewed about perceived personal security, use of new technology, and demographic factors. The sample was drawn with a multi-stage sampling procedure. In 2008, another survey was conducted with a sample of 217 journalists who were identified with the same multi-stage sampling procedure. In Hong Kong, three surveys were conducted among journalists working in mainstream daily newspapers and the news departments of television and radio broadcasters. The questionnaires of all three surveys, which were conducted in 1996, 2001, and 2006, focused on journalists' job satisfaction, professional norms, and beliefs about ethical behavior. In Indonesia, two surveys were conducted.

The first survey was fielded between August 2001 and February 2002 with a sample of 385 journalists. The sample was drawn from the provinces of Jakarta and Yogyakarta. The second study is based on a sample of 100 journalists working in 20 news organizations, who were interviewed between November 2007 and January 2008. In Israel, three surveys were conducted: the 2002 ($N = 209$) and 2004 studies ($N = 200$) are based on stratified samples of journalists working at Hebrew-language news outlets and alternative media targeting specific populations in Israel. The 2008 survey ($N = 333$) also included journalists working for local radio stations, foreign-language and financial media, free newspapers, and online media. The focus in all three surveys was on journalists' working conditions, their professional values and ethics, and their perceptions of the Israeli news media. In Switzerland, three surveys were conducted: the first survey ($N = 449$) contacted journalists working at private broadcasting stations and was carried out between November 2006 and January 2007. The second survey ($N = 657$) targeted journalists working in the public broadcasting corporation and was carried out between September and October 2007. The third survey ($N = 1403$) interviewed journalists working in the print media and was conducted between June and July 2008. All three studies used comparable questionnaires, concentrating on aspects such as the journalists' employment situation, role definitions, job satisfaction, and socio-demographics. In the United States, two surveys were conducted: in 2002, a representative survey of 1149 journalists was conducted focusing on journalists' perceptions of their professional roles and values, job satisfaction, and demographic background factors. The second study was based on 400 journalists who participated in the 2002 survey and were interviewed again in 2007.

2. The questions used to assess "job satisfaction" varied slightly from country to country: France: "very happy" to be a journalist; Hong Kong: those scoring 5 on a five-point Likert scale; South Korea: those scoring 9 and 10 on a 11-point satisfaction scale; Israel: "strongly agree" to "I enjoy going to work every day."
3. The questions used to assess "perceived job autonomy" varied slightly from country to country: Indonesia: "strongly agree" to "I am allowed to take part in decisions that affect my work"; Singapore: percentage of journalists saying they have "almost complete freedom" (8.3 percent) and "considerable freedom" (41.7 percent); Sweden: percentage of journalists answering "almost complete freedom" to the question "How much freedom do you usually have in selecting the stories you work on?"; UAE: journalists saying they are "almost completely free" to select a story to cover; Israel: journalists saying they "strongly agree" with the statement "I feel that my superiors allow me to operate freely."
4. "Importance of job autonomy" is measured as percentage of journalists saying that job autonomy is a "very important" aspect of their job.

REFERENCES

Bardoel, Jo. 1996. "Beyond Journalism: A Profession between Information Society and Civil Society." *European Journal of Communication* 11 (3): 283–302.

Barrett, Grace H. 1984. "Job Satisfaction among Newspaperwomen." *Journalism Quarterly* 61 (3): 593–599.

Beam, Randal A. 1990. "Journalism Professionalism as an Organizational-level Concept." *Journalism Monographs* 121: 1–43.

Blumler, Jay G., Jack M. McLeod, and Karl E. Rosengren. 1992. *Comparatively Speaking: Communication and Culture across Space and Time*. Newbury Park, CA: Sage.

Bowman, James. 1996. "A Pretense of Professionalism." *New Criterion* 15 (4): 55–61.

Cokley, John, Deb H. Wenger, Mitch Wenger, and Jessica McBride. 2011. "US, Europe Journalism Competencies Wish-lists Out of Step but Some Alignments Evident." Paper presented to the Journalism Education Association of Australia annual conference, Adelaide, November 28–30.

Cooper-Chen, Anne. 1997. *Mass Communication in Japan*. Ames: Iowa State University Press.

Cremedas, Michael, and Suzanne Lysak. 2011. "'New Media' Skills Competency Expected of TV Reporters and Producers: A Survey." *Electronic News* 5 (1): 41–59.

Deprez, Annelore, and Karin Raeymaeckers. 2012. "A Longitudinal Study of Job Satisfaction among Flemish Professional Journalists." *Journalism and Mass Communication* 2 (1): 1–15.

Deuze, Mark. 2002. *Journalists in the Netherlands*. Amsterdam: Aksant.

Deuze, Mark. 2005. "What Is Journalism? Professional Identity and Ideology of Journalists Reconsidered." *Journalism* 6 (4): 442–464.

Deuze, Mark. 2007. *Media Work*. Cambridge: Polity Press.

Feldman, Ofer. 1993. *Politics and the News Media in Japan*. Ann Arbor: University of Michigan Press.

Glasser, Theodore L. 1992. "Professionalism and the Derision of Diversity: The Case of the Education of Journalists." *Journal of Communication* 42 (2): 131–140.

Hall, Jim. 2001. *Online Journalism: A Critical Primer*. London: Longman.

Hallin, Daniel. 2000. "Commercialism and the Professionalism in the American News Media." In *Mass Media and Society*, edited by James Curran and Michael Gurevitch, 218–237. London: Arnold.

Hallin, Daniel C., and Paolo Mancini. 2004. *Comparing Media Systems*. New York: Cambridge University Press.

Köcher, Renate. 1986. "Bloodhounds or Missionaries: Role Definitions of German and British Journalists." *European Journal of Communication* 1: 43–64.

Lawrence, Arthur. 1903. *Journalism As a Profession*. London: Hodder and Stoughton.

Man Chan, Joseph, Zhongdang Pan, and Francis L. F. Lee. 2004. "Professional Aspirations and Job Satisfaction: Chinese Journalists at a Time of Change in the Media." *Journalism & Mass Communication Quarterly* 81 (2): 254–273.

Pavlik, John V. 1999. "New Media and News: Implications for the Future of Journalism." *New Media and Society* 1 (1): 54–59.

Pollard, George. 1995. "Job Satisfaction among News Workers: The Influence of Professionalism, Perceptions of Organizational Structure and Social Attributes." *Journalism & Mass Communication Quarterly* 72: 682–697.

Powers, Angela. 1991. "The Effect of Leadership Behavior on Job Satisfaction and Goal Agreement and Attainment in Local TV News." *Journalism Quarterly* 68 (4): 772–780.

Reinardy, Scott. 2007. "Satisfaction vs. Sacrifice: Sports Editors Assess the Influences of Life Issues on Job Satisfaction." *Journalism & Mass Communication Quarterly* 84 (1): 105–121.

Splichal, Slavko, and Colin Sparks. 1994. *Journalists for the 21st Century*. Norwood, NJ: Ablex.

Stamm, Keith, and Doug Underwood. 1993. "The Relationship of Job Satisfaction to Newsroom Policy Changes." *Journalism & Mass Communication Quarterly* 70 (3): 528–541.

Takeshita, Toshio, and Masamichi Ida. 2009. "Political Communication in Japan." In *Political Communication in Asia*, edited by Lars Willnat and Annette Aw, 154–175. New York: Routledge.

Tamam, Ezhar, Sony J. Raj, and Manimaran Govindasamy. 2012. "Malaysian Journalists." In *The Global Journalist in the 21st Century*, edited by David H. Weaver and Lars Willnat, 78–90. New York: Routledge.

Tietjen, Mark A., and Robert M. Myers. 1998. "Motivation and Job Satisfaction." *Management Decision* 36 (4): 226–231.

Tumber, Howard. 2001. "Democracy in the Information Age: The Role of the Fourth Estate in Cyberspace." *Information, Communication and Society* 4 (1): 95–112.

Tumber, Howard, and Michael Bromley. 1998. "Virtual Soundbites: Political Communication in Cyberspace." *Media, Culture and Society* 20: 159–167.

Tumber, Howard, and Marina Prentoulis. 2005. "Journalism and the Making of a Profession." In *Making Journalists*, edited by Hugo de Burgh, 58–74. New York: Routledge.

Ward, Stephen J. A. 2009. "Journalism Ethics." In *The Handbook of Journalism Studies*, edited by Karin Wahl-Jorgensen and Thomas Hanitzsch, 295–309. New York: Routledge.

Weaver, David H. 1998. *The Global Journalist: News People around the World*. Cresskill, NJ: Hampton Press.

Weaver, David H., Randal A. Beam, Bonnie J. Brownlee, Paul S. Voakes, and G. Cleveland Wilhoit. 2007. *The American Journalist in the 21st Century: U.S. News People at the Dawn of a New Millennium*. Mahwah, NJ: Lawrence Erlbaum.

Weaver, David H., and G. Cleveland Wilhoit. 1986. *The American Journalist: A Portrait of U.S. News People and their Work*. Bloomington: Indiana University Press.

Weaver, David H., and G. Cleveland Wilhoit. 1996. *The American Journalist in the 1990s: U.S. News People at the End of an Era*. Mahwah, NJ: Erlbaum.

Weaver, David H., and Lars Willnat. 2012. *The Global Journalist in the 21st Century*. New York: Routledge.

Zhu, Jian-Hua, David H. Weaver, Ven-Hwei Lo, Chongshan Chen, and Wei Wu. 1997. "Individual, Organizational and Societal Influences on Media Role Perceptions: A Comparative Study of Journalists in China, Taiwan, and the United States." *Journalism & Mass Communication Quarterly* 74 (1): 84–96.

CULTURE CLASH

International media training and the difficult adoption of Western journalism practices among Indonesian radio journalists

Nurhaya Muchtar and **Thomas Hanitzsch**

International media training has become popular in post-New Order Indonesia. Educational organizations have focused on training radio journalists, reflecting the accessibility of radio stations across the nation. This study investigated the training effectiveness and consequent adoption of Western journalism practices in the context of Indonesian radio journalism. Five focus groups were conducted in five Indonesian cities with distinctive media markets, populations, and city sizes. Findings illustrate that the adoption and dissemination of training materials were made more difficult by the widely differing values and backgrounds of journalists as well as a lack of funding from radio stations.

Introduction

Since 1996, international media education/donor agencies have been offering media training in Indonesia to improve democracy and civil society. Media training falls under the "Democracy Assistance" heading, which is the largest part of foreign aid due to its primary role in developing civil society, strengthening legislative bodies and political parties, and increasing transparency—an essential element in bolstering democracy and asserting the rule of law (Bollen, Paxton, and Morishima 2005).

Training organizations mostly hired journalism professors or media professionals from Western countries such as Germany, Australia, Canada, the United States and the United Kingdom. The Nieman Foundation for Journalism at Harvard University reported that some of the trainers claimed they had achieved their goals, however they added that it failed to change journalism practices in recipient countries because of existing standards and values (Valentine 2005).

This article explores the challenges faced by journalists in trying to adopt the journalistic practices advocated by these international media education organizations in the context of Indonesia, especially in the area of radio journalism. Modernization and diffusion theory are used to understand how journalism values were shared by trainers and challenged by journalism trainees. Our findings show that adoption of Western journalism practices was hampered at least temporarily by various factors, most notably a clash of professional values during training in addition to tough competition and the high costs of news production. This paper highlights the different value systems that the trainers brought to the training and which slowed the move toward Western journalism practices. The adoption process was also held back by incompatibilities between local realities and the normative underpinnings of the teaching.

Literature Review

The Rise of Radio Journalism in Indonesia

Indonesia has been a major recipient country of international media education due to the political upheaval that followed the collapse of the Suharto regime in 1998 as well as an unprecedented media boom in subsequent years which triggered a sudden demand for qualified media professionals (Hanitzsch 2005). The Indonesia that emerged from the wreckage of the old regime was in a very unstable condition, reflecting a severe economic crisis, a political legacy of authoritarianism, and ethnic and religious conflicts across the vast archipelago.

In this context, international media training organizations and donor agencies concentrated their efforts on radio stations and radio journalists given the accessibility of radio stations across the country. During the transition years people very much relied on radio news and information, but radio journalists were insufficiently equipped for this task due to a long history of media restrictions. For years, General Suharto's New Order government had kept a tight rein on radio stations, especially in the area of news production. In 1974, for example, through its Information, Transportation and Justice departments, the government told stations to refrain from both independent news reporting and broadcasting of foreign news programs, and prohibited them from engaging in news production or political activities on threat of having their licenses revoked (Susanto 1974).

The government also demanded that the stations' educational and informational programs adhere to the State's official philosophy, known as *Pancasila*, which was derived from *development journalism*, also called *positive journalism*. The concept was initially adopted by developing countries as a way to reject Western ideas and to foster economic, social and cultural progress. Stations were expected to relay State radio news bulletins about 15–17 times a day, as well as other State programs such as those detailing presidential visits or ceremonies, which could take up another five hours every day (Lindsay 1997). In addition, stations had to dedicate 10 percent of their programming to public service (Susanto 1974, 235). In order to make sure all stations complied with this rule, the government set up in every province a special body made up of police and military officers as well as officials from the departments of Information and Justice. This special body had the power to regulate, monitor, and control stations, and to revoke their licenses if they were thought to be breaking the law (Sen 2003). Furthermore, the government used private radio associations as an added means of control (Sen and Hill 2006).

With the New Order government losing its grip on power in the late 1980s/early 1990s, restrictions started to let up. The rising middle classes, Islamic groups, and dissident political leaders began clamoring for government openness and transparency. Some stations saw an opportunity to become an opinion vehicle. They produced programs such as talk-shows whose format included a host, a number of experts, and, crucially, call-in audience participation. Radio Suara Surabaya (SS), for example, changed its format in 1983 to news and talk due to the owner's belief that radio should be a bridge between the State and the people (Soekomihardjo 2003). Only a few stations followed this path, partly because many had close ties with the President (Sen 2003). According to Jurriens (2007), this effort should be credited for its role in forming public opinion—an essential building block of any civil society and democracy. Involving the audience in radio talk-show programs was also an attempt to create legitimate local news and information despite the absence of journalism skills and limited news production facilities (Jurriens 2007, 119; Sen and Hill 2006).

This era was considered the earliest stage of development of radio journalism in Indonesia (Jurriens 2007). Other stations continued relaying news bulletins from State radio. As an alternative, they broadcast news flashes that were about 3–15 minutes long at any time of the day. Both talk shows and news flashes began to increase radio's popularity (Sen 2003). As an increasing number of stations took this path, government control decreased, in part because of a lack of monitoring equipment. For example, in Jogjakarta in 1996, the authorities had only one receiver available to check whether the 15 local broadcasters actually relayed news bulletins from the State-owned Radio Republik Indonesia (RRI) (Sen 2003). The government's decision to legalize news programs on commercial radio stations the following year also played a pivotal role (Kitley 2000). Thus, all of these factors—in a context of social and political instability fuelled by religious and ethnic conflicts and a brutal economic crisis—not only increased the popularity of radio stations, but also supported the birth of community radio as an alternative voice for the people (Gazali 2002).

Around that time international organizations stepped in, offering media training to radio stations. Initially, training content mainly focused on basic journalism skills and targeted music hosts, sales and marketing staff, station managers, and even owners. A reason for this was the absence of news departments in radio stations due to government regulations (Sen and Hill 2006) and the consequent skills shortage in this field. Soon after that, content diversified and extended to election coverage, peace reporting, HIV/AIDS coverage, as well as bird flu and environment reporting. The training basically pertained to a combination of journalism skills tied to selected topics relating to these themes. Most of the activities incorporated technical training, such as using digital audio recorders in field reports and editing pieces with digital audio software (Kumar 2006a).

Previous research on media training highlighted several challenges faced by international trainers. These challenges often limited the sustainability of the training outcomes. In a case study on the implementation of media training in Indonesia, Kumar (2006b) and his team specifically looked at a single training provider, Internews—one of the largest training organizations in Indonesia, which serves a number of partner stations. They found that there was some duplication in training, as well as a communication gap between foreign trainers and local participants. Although participants indeed valued new ideas and approaches, they said that the contents could have been better tailored to their needs. Some of these needs can be related to how they see their roles in society.

Through interviews with 15 trainers, Muchtar and Haley (2008) found that some problems in imparting skills to participants were due to ambiguous information provided by the training organization about their trainees. Many times, trainers said that they had very limited information and were left alone, which made it difficult for them to achieve their goals. The trainers believed that understanding a culture should be a prerequisite as it can help prepare the right material for the participants, choose the best approach, create trust, and support the transfer of knowledge and skills. They said that training organizers should have been the ones to provide such information as they had been in the country longer than any trainers.

LaMay (2007) conducted a study on media assistance in Indonesia, specifically focusing on assistance received by Radio Jurnal Perempuan [Women's Journal Radio] and

Kantor Berita Radio 68H [Radio News Agency 68H]—an internet-based network that feeds news and information to radio stations across Indonesia. The former created weekly feature programs and provided them freely to radio stations all over the country, while the latter provided different kinds of news programs from live reports, news bulletins, and feature stories. Both organizations received initial funding from USAID. LaMay argued that the editorial mission of Radio Jurnal Perempuan raised concerns over the journalist's relationship to civil society and the kind of journalism suited to the needs of democratizing societies. The fact that the organization depends on external funding also created ambiguities about objectivity and editorial independence. LaMay's findings describe many problems related to media training not only in Indonesia but around the world. He argues that there was a "joint problem" of economic viability and editorial quality from the point of view of journalists in developing countries. This was due to the fact that the ultimate goal of training and other assistance was to create a free and independent media. For such a goal to be achieved, however, media houses had to be economically viable, otherwise other entities were bound to take them over and return things to how they were in the bad old days of censorship.

A few managers in training organizations reported that funding availability often dictated media training activities. In Indonesia, media training was a high priority between 1998 and 2003. However, it declined along with decreasing funding. This clearly shows that availability or unavailability of funding can have a powerful impact on the teaching process. The training organizations pointed to the fast growth of international development work as one of the reasons behind difficulties with both funding and project implementation. They also said that competition between training organizations made cooperation among them nearly impossible. Cooperation and coordination were usually possible only in regions where facilities were at a bare minimum, such as Afghanistan and Iraq. Anywhere else, self-interest tended to kick in and preclude any cooperation between large organizations (Muchtar 2010).

Indonesian Journalists

Previous studies of journalists in Indonesia focused on their educational backgrounds and value systems. Hanitzsch (2005) conducted a survey of 385 Indonesian journalists to determine how they had acquired their journalistic skills. He found that most of the working journalists owed their skills and techniques to internal training from the media institution they worked for. Pintak and Setiyono (2011) conducted a similar study involving 600 journalists across the country. They noted that an increasing number of journalists earned a college degree prior to working as journalists. They also found that Indonesian journalists appeared to have different priorities in reporting the news. Further, they discovered that Indonesian journalists view their roles as agents of change: supporting political change, encouraging civic engagement, upholding religious values, entertaining the public, and transforming society. This is certainly different from the professional and cultural values that underpin journalism in Western countries.

Regarding news values, Romano (2003) found that government restrictions have profoundly shaped journalists' ways of thinking and the practice of journalism in Indonesia. Most journalists thought of themselves as "keepers" rather than "watchdogs" of Society. This journalism culture was partly influenced by the notion of *Pancasila Press*, which was derived from the idea of "development journalism." The concept was initially adopted by several developing countries as a rejection of Western ideas and a way to encourage the media to concentrate on positive aspects when covering national development and security issues as well as social and cultural problems (Edeani 1993; Richstad 2000; Romano 2005; Wong 2004). In the context of Indonesia, this was explicitly acknowledged by President Suharto (Soeharto 1989), who ruled the country for 30 years. This journalism culture not only influenced media professionals but people at large, especially those close to power.

Most studies by Indonesian media practitioners focused on print and television journalists. Radio journalists were often considered a special breed in the context of Indonesia's media system because they were less acquainted with journalism and mostly functioned as entertainers. For them, media training was often essential to fill the gap left by Indonesian higher education.

Theoretical Framework

The effectiveness of knowledge transfer through media training can be analyzed using modernization theory and diffusion of innovation theory. Modernization theory, which emerged in the 1950s, refers primarily to economic change and the shift from a primitive, agrarian, and traditionalist society to an industrialized, urbanized, and modern one. The Western perspective on social change is "explicitly or implicitly understood to be synonymous to development" (Hedebro 1982, 19). The theory also states that transfer of knowledge and technology from developed nations is a necessary element for developing nations to achieve economic growth as soon as possible (Peet and Hartwick 1999). Critics of modernization theory argued that this model is ethnocentric, ideologically biased and mostly unable to produce the desired outcomes. While in many developed countries economic growth has indeed improved the material living conditions of parts of the population, it has not necessarily led to social change, democratic governance and a more even distribution of resources (Fair 1989; Rogers 1976; Sussman and Lent 1991). Despite these limitations, the modernization paradigm thrived in academic literature until the late 1980s (Fair 1989).

One of the strong opponents of modernization theory is Everett Rogers, who originated the diffusion of innovation theory based on his studies in agriculture and rural sociology in the 1960s. Rogers (1971) defines diffusion as the process in which an innovation spreads over time among the members of a social system through certain communication channels. The diffusion of new ideas includes four major characteristics: time, innovation, communication channels, and social systems (Rogers 1971). Unlike modernization theorists, Rogers argued that diffusion of innovations should incorporate a bottom-up approach in order to produce sustainable outcomes.

Rogers' theory of diffusion did not really cover training but focused on the natural adoption process. Training to facilitate adoption has been used by many industries—including media institutions—as an approach to improve their staff's professional skills and enlarge their customer base. However, some media institutions could not provide adequate professional training owing to their limited resources. In addition, this was mostly the case in developing countries that restricted freedom of the press and freedom of expression. This situation caused many media institutions in developing countries to rely on formal education only, which often failed to address the needs of the industry.

Studies of media training showed that a common approach used by international media training organizations was of the top-down variety: trainers imparted a shared set of news values and practices which did not necessarily meet the needs of the trainees (Kumar 2006b; LaMay 2007; Muchtar and Haley 2008). This indicates that despite strong criticisms from academics and practitioners alike, modernization theory still infuses much of international media training. In 2002, Napoli conducted a case study of media training in Albania, which, just like Indonesia, has received much professional training from Western organizations. While Albanian journalists were taught to produce high-quality news stories, the training did not take hold because of conflicting backgrounds: trainers came from societies that practice objective journalism, while the trainees worked in a country where development journalism was dominant, with stories being expected to support economic development as promoted by the government.

Such studies highlight the disconnect between a training model steeped in Western normative values and the concrete needs of the trainees, which inevitably leads to limited sustainability in training outcomes. The fact that only minimal information is gleaned from trainees during the training process creates problems for trainers and trainees alike. Trainers tended to prepare training materials based on their previous experience, while trainees came in expecting to acquire skills relevant to their actual needs on the job. In addition, we believe that a number of issues need to be addressed with respect to the transfer of journalistic ideology (Golding 1977). First, does international media training indeed lead to the adoption of Western journalism practices in Indonesian radio stations? If not, what were the challenges to adoption? Furthermore, this study can extend the diffusion of innovation theory in the area of international media training. Based on the studies and findings above, we believe there is a need to conduct a study to determine the trainees' perspectives on media training as well as the effectiveness of the diffusion process on radio journalism. We therefore advance the following research questions:

RQ1: How did trainers impart their knowledge of journalism to Indonesian journalists?

RQ2: What are the main challenges faced by radio professionals during the adoption process?

Method

For the purpose of this study, the first author of this paper conducted five focus group discussions with five to eight participants in each group. The aim was to study how journalists as a group viewed training impact on their skills and the development of radio journalism in general. Focus group discussions can yield rich information when participants interact with each other by agreeing or disagreeing about the selected topic. Thus, focus groups can bring more perspectives through the involvement of individuals and group dynamics (Hakim 2000, 35). When a course has been over for a while, focus group discussions can help refresh memories of the training and its impact on individuals, groups, and their workplaces.

Focus group discussions were conducted in five Indonesian cities: Jakarta, Jogjakarta, Surabaya, Makassar, and Palu. The first three are located on Java island, Indonesia's largest media market, the other two on the island of Sulawesi. Each area has distinctive characteristics: Jakarta and Surabaya are large metropolitan cities, and the others are smaller in terms of population and market size. Selecting a number of cities was necessary to understand the social realities that influence adoption of radio journalism skills by radio journalists in the various regions of the country. Because some training organizations were no longer active by the time the research was conducted, we contacted the Indonesia Private Broadcast Radio Association (PRSSNI)—which worked with many training organizations in the past—in the hope of identifying participants in these training sessions. In addition, we discussed the matter with several of the remaining media training organizations. The researcher prepared a discussion guide to moderate the conversation, while in some cases the participants introduced new topics that functioned as an extension of other participants' opinions. The focus group discussions were digitally recorded and answers were translated into English during the transcription process.

Findings

There were altogether 30 journalists who participated in the focus group discussions. Each group consisted of five to eight participants. Journalists worked mainly for radio stations, but many of them had other jobs as well. Average professional experience was 14 years. Those who had worked for more than 10 years said they used to work mainly as radio hosts before their stations started producing local news. Most of the participants reported that they had attended more than three training workshops held by international training organizations. In Makassar and Palu, each participant had attended more than a dozen training sessions.

Three topics came up in every discussion: the benefits of training; the challenges in adoption; and dissemination of training materials. Other topics were mentioned in some areas but not in others for various reasons: number of training programs attended, popularity of news programs, and station size.

Benefits of Training

One of the programs attended by almost all participants was basic journalism training. The main distinction between this and other types of training was that the participants gathered news in the field and produced news stories with equipment provided by the training organizers. In a few cases, trainers assisted with fieldwork and production exercises. The participants said that this approach introduced them to new radio journalism ideas, skills, and techniques. As for thematic training, selection of themes was often determined by where the participants lived as well as popular issues in their regions. In Palu, for example, most radio journalists had received conflict and peace reporting training due to proximity to the ethnic and religious conflict site in Poso, while the Jakarta and Surabaya journalists had received more advanced journalism training such as investigative journalism or environmental reporting. Some themes included bird flu reporting, conflict reporting, and election reporting. All included a skills training component.

Depending on their interests and job at the time they joined the training, participants had diverging ideas about its main benefits. Most of them mentioned writing, and a number mentioned editing and production, especially feature production. A Surabaya journalist said:

> You know at that time, what we mainly did was live reporting, sometimes with sound bites, other times without. When they introduced me to a new skill in feature production, I finally knew the power of features especially in building ambiance, which is in line with the strength of radio as a medium that can touch on imagination and feeling. When told how to produce features, for example on some serious incident, we were able to enrich them with human interests stories.

A journalist from Makassar agreed:

> I remember most of the skill training, from field report to choosing a story angle, from fieldwork to writing a script. And of course the number one rule in radio: "one idea, one sentence". Choice of words is crucial—better simple and meaningful than complicated and rambling.

Only a few journalists commented on other topics:

> For me it is the concept of balance. Another thing is related to tips or tricks. That it is better to present the right information than to beat everyone to a meaningless story. Better right than fast. I guess, I can't say much about skills. Maybe because I use them every day, so it becomes usual.

Prior to their first training experience, many of the journalists admitted that they followed the way print and TV journalists did their work—not only how they wrote their stories but also the way they presented them. A journalist from Jogjakarta said the training gave him a new understanding of radio:

> I used to have a limited understanding of news in radio or radio journalism. Maybe it's because I used to work for campus media. I mean I used different styles. Until the BBC trained us I thought the right one was the style used by RRI [the state-run radio station]. So I started comparing different products. As I learned and attended more training workshops, I finally realized that radio journalism is basically different from print journalism.

All radio journalists seemed to agree that they learned more about writing, which they recalled in different terms such as the KISS concept, which abbreviates the injunction to "Keep it Short and Simple," and the "writing for the ear" rule. A Jakarta journalist who claimed to spend a lot of time on every interview described how training helped make his work more effective:

> I learned to look for an answer, because the answer does not necessarily become a good sound bite. So what I did was—when I heard a good sound bite during the interview, I sometimes repeated or paraphrased it, because a good sound bite would help me identify an angle for my story. That's what I did and what I shared with other participants as well.

Challenges in Adoption

Most participants had tried to adopt training materials in their workplaces. However, certain practices learned during training were difficult to put into practice, a problem that had much to do with the trainers. Most organizations recruited their trainers in countries that were very different from those where the training was offered. They were either working journalists or journalism (or media) professors in their home countries or in international settings. Their backgrounds generally influenced the kind of material that was shared and how it was shared with the participants. Trainers introduced a range of radio broadcasting skills and knowledge that their trainees had never heard of before. A Jogjakarta reporter who currently works as both station manager and journalism professor aptly summarized the trainees' general sentiment towards their foreign trainers:

> I see that the different culture that the trainers bring is interesting to know. For example, issues related to deadlines. During training, we thought we didn't have to finish the assignment. But it turned out that we had to finish it in a very limited time. Once, I joined a three-day training course. The first day was for trainers to give us training material, on the second day we covered a story, and we finished the production on the third day. Those tight deadlines made us understand how foreign reporters work. So they taught us not only training material (journalism techniques) but also journalism culture. I think this is important.

In response to their comments, the participants related it to their work experience in adopting training material. They said that each trainer brought examples from their home countries, and that they were different from other trainers from whom they had received training before. Some of these materials were not related at all to the Indonesian context.

Different trainers, different approaches, and different examples of training contents on journalism left some journalists confused about what and how they should apply the training in their daily work. In the end, the trainees learned to understand the trainers and their origins in order to understand the lessons shared during the training. A journalist from Jogjakarta described how the trainers' origins and cultural backgrounds affected the way he grasped information from the training:

> Once, we had a trainer from Germany. Some of his materials and examples were drawn from his experiences in his country and Australia. You see, our audience has a different social background. People in these countries might speak right to the point, but our people love beating around the bush. I admit the training material is very good, but it should be based on the society we serve.

The second challenge is the training content. Some journalists said that thematic training was more challenging to understand and to apply. A Palu journalist, who had covered many stories in conflict areas in Poso, described his experience in adopting new skills:

> Most of the things we were taught by the trainers were excellent. But when we tried to adopt and adapt them to our job, it just didn't work. One reason was that content was based on *their* point of view.

Furthermore, journalists from Makassar and Palu said:

> We had trainers from various countries, not only the US and the UK but also Germany and France. The main problem is that when they taught conflict coverage, they used cases that happened in Europe. And things here are very different—we have a different media system, different regulations. So their suggestions on the best way for journalists to do conflict reporting do not really apply out here.

Some participants pointed out the flaws of the training in conflict and peace reporting.

> I joined peace journalism training, and there were a few things that I could not put into practice. I was told that when we went to a conflict area, we needed to be in a certain place. Well, I couldn't do that, it's simply too difficult. I was hit many times, by stones or

> other things. You know, you can't be safe doing that. So whatever they [the trainers] said worked in their home country does not necessarily work here in Indonesia. For example, people or the police here do not treat journalists the way they do in the US or elsewhere.

The third challenge with respect to adoption pertains to use of technology. Journalists said most trainers used sophisticated gadgets and technologies that the participants did not have during the training. Since most participants in the early days of training had no equipment experience or understanding of radio journalism, they found it difficult to understand the equipment. Most participants did not ascribe this to inadequate preparation on the part of the trainers, but to insufficient information about the local situation. They wished the trainers had known and understood the general conditions of local journalism and the local culture prior to the training. A Jakarta participant said:

> We needed people who understood and had experience in the local situation. If they used to work for the BBC, understood the local situation and spoke the language—so much the better. Why waste valuable time with translation?

The last challenge was the nature of the journalism training, which seemed somewhat detached from management-related training. This created some sort of cognitive dissonance among journalists and their managers. During the journalism training, journalists said trainers emphasized objective reporting, while managers were trained in profit making with no real connection to news programming. Most journalists in Palu reported that the knowledge gap between journalists and managers had even widened after the trainings.

> When we received the training, we didn't talk about business. We were told that we should be independent and that media should be independent. This is hard because when we talk about business in a media context, they look at everything that might bring profit. They [the managers] are more interested in programs that can generate audience. I believe this is the case in all media.

Most journalists expressed similar ideas. They were aware that managers and journalists had their own specific goals in the training, but they said they wished training organizers had created more awareness of the importance of news programs. In addition, the Jakarta and Palu journalists said that both managers and journalists should attend the same training programs. A Jakarta journalist said:

> Journalism training should discuss how to create good news programs that generate money. If print and TV can sell news programs, why can't the radio do the same thing? I know that radio stations in Jakarta can do this, but what about stations in other regions?

In addition, a Palu journalist said that an integrated training approach should give their managers journalism training as well.

> I think it's ironic that new reporters should take basic journalism. I believe we need to change this. A station manager needs to take it. They need to know everything in the station, including news programs. We have a problem here, inasmuch most of our managers know news through learning by doing. We, the staff, learned from the experts, something that was totally new. They [the managers] learned eighties-style journalism, while what we learned was steeped in the 2000s. This is really quite serious because it created a communication problem between us. Of course, they would never admit that they don't understand, but clearly, their understanding of news is totally different from ours.

Dissemination and Adoption

Most journalists who attended training felt motivated to bring new ideas and change to their stations. However, many of them were discouraged by management and owners. Jogjakarta journalists said they understood why their station managers did not welcome new ideas that might drastically change their operations. Other journalists said that in the long run, the excitement gained from the training could lead to frustration and even disagreements with the station manager, which impacted on radio operations:

> It's all because of company policy. Many times we found ourselves in conflict with the policy of our stations. Trainers often imparted journalism techniques that could never be implemented in our stations—because such techniques and values clashed with station policy. I do believe that training creates better quality journalists, but that didn't lead to better media in Indonesia because when talking about media development we tend to refer to the media [as institution], not to individual journalists. We have seen more and more great reporters, but as an institution, the media stagnate.

Apart from gaining a new understanding of journalism techniques and knowledge, most participants were expected to spread their knowledge among their colleagues back home. Depending on where they worked and what their jobs were at the time, some of the participants indicated that they had to share the material through brief presentations to their colleagues, along with the results of the co-production made as part of the training. Some made one- to two-hour presentations to their colleagues. Others had to use the training material in their work, and then present examples to their colleagues. Others said they did not have to do anything at all. Only Jogjakarta journalists reported that they did not share any of their new know-how with their colleagues because there were no opportunities provided by their managers. They said their stations' formats were mainly music, with a smattering of news programs. A Jogjakarta journalist explained why he did not share training materials and did not use what he had learnt:

> No, they didn't provide a space to share. Besides, at that time most stations were not serious with their news and journalism work. So most of us who came to the training were not there as representatives of our institutions.

A few participants in Jakarta, who were working as local trainers, said that dissemination of training information was still limited. They had seen some improvements in radio journalism with respect to some techniques but not in other areas:

> What I have seen really developed is the ability to use Cool Edit Pro. They're [former journalism trainees] really good. It really made a difference. In terms of writing, it is good, it is improving. But with regards to other skills, no . . . it is still bad. You know why? Because there is no knowledge transfer. Those who attended the training did not share the information with their colleagues. So I have to say that journalism in Indonesia is still in a rut. And as for news programs, I think most people still believe that news does not generate money, so they don't care to make use of what they learned.

Most participants said they chose to adopt new practices in their daily work, depending on their responsibilities. They explained that they applied the training in their work gradually as long as it did not create a major change. They chose a personal and individual approach, incorporating new skills in their existing work rather than creating new programs. For example, those who worked as hosts said they made good use of their new writing and interviewing skills. Two of the most popular skills for journalists to adopt were writing and multi-track audio editing using the Cool Edit Pro software. Prior to the training workshops many radio stations—especially those located outside Java—were still editing sound manually well into the 1990s. A Makassar journalist described thematic training as one of the most difficult skills to adopt:

> We used the training material in our work because much of the material was relevant and helped us in our work as journalists. As for thematic training, it takes time. It all depends. If the theme is related to current issues, of course we are interested to cover it. We have to admit, we were so passionate, at least after a week of training, but after that it all depends on the situation.

Most journalists said that some of them had had opportunities to foster change by creating new programs. Having realized office policy would prevent him from introducing major changes, a Jogjakarta journalist chose a different tack:

> I think what matters is to actually do something with the training material, even if it's small and adapted to our station's format. We made drastic changes once or twice in terms of style and content. But overall, what we have been doing is try and present in a different way those same news stories that other stations have. At times we try to find fresh news, and at other times we use what we have but try to go more in-depth.

A Jakarta journalist who worked for a station in Jogjakarta described how he gradually wove the training materials into his work:

> I do believe change is a process. As you know there were so many training programs here. So what I did was try and compile it all in a certain way, which I dubbed in my "news-radio version." I didn't make any [post-training] change because the theories were not applicable, possibly because the trainers were foreigners. For example, they told us that we should read the news as if we were telling a story. It is difficult, you know. It sounds easy for them maybe but we tended to follow our TV hosts.

Some participants changed the way they created news bulletins. This happened after a number of trainers had been coming in every day for about a week to work with a station's new staff members. This in-house setting afforded them many opportunities to talk with managers and other staff and explain the benefits of the new skills. A few participants in Palu said they produced news bulletins for about six months before completely stopping.

In the early days of reform many stations broadcast news in a format based on their segmentation and positioning. However, stations often could not air a given story because their owner would not allow it. A journalist from Palu, whose manager was involved in local business and politics, said:

> There are a few owners who get involved in politics. So, we can't report objectively because it might be counterproductive for our owners. There was a time when I wanted to report a corruption issue. I really wanted to report it because the public has a right to know, but I couldn't because the station's owner asked me not to.

Discussion and Conclusions

In the years following the collapse of the Suharto regime, in 1998, Indonesia experienced an unparalleled media boom. Consequently, demand for qualified journalists skyrocketed. The country's media system was shifting from a closed and authoritarian system with limited press freedom to democratic structures of mass participation and an unprecedented independence of the media from state intervention. Mostly due to a lack of domestic experience and educational resources, Indonesia became one of the major recipient countries of international media training during the transition years.

International training organizations generally employed instructors from Western countries such as Australia, Canada, Germany, and the United Kingdom—in other words people whose backgrounds were completely at odds with those of the journalists they were to train. A major challenge therefore lay in the need to find a common ground between the Western experience and values of the instructors and international training organizations, on the one hand, and the complex realities of Indonesia's multi-ethnic and multi-religious society, on the other hand. And this challenge was mostly lost as the contradictions between the normative underpinnings of international media training and the practical constraints in the field substantially hampered the adoption of news skills and knowledge.

A central and very telling finding of this study is that even fairly recent media training activities in Indonesia often used a top-down approach. Instructors tried to "transplant" Western professional values and practices into incompatible soil, using training materials that did not necessarily address the needs of the trainees. This result ties in with evidence from previous research. It seems that despite strong criticism from academics and practitioners, international media training still very much relies on a modernization theory perspective.

The disconnect between the normative approach of international media trainers and the concrete needs of Indonesian journalists becomes obvious when one looks at the kind of training material used during the instructions. Trainers often brought up examples from their home countries that were in no way related to the Indonesian context. The skills and knowledge conveyed in these media trainings were then of fairly limited use to the journalists, for a number of reasons. First, while the training was based on concrete examples and cases, instructors often failed to take into account the very specific nature of Indonesia's media system. This was especially problematic for conflict reporting training. The structural conditions of Indonesia's media system, its regulatory contexts and socio-cultural conditions in the field often worked against the well-meaning Western trainers. Furthermore, teaching materials frequently referred to journalistic techniques and values that could not be implemented in practice as they conflicted with the editorial policies and organizational imperatives of many Indonesian radio stations. As a result, while many trainees thought highly of what they had learned, they had to recognize that putting it into practice was simply impossible.

A second important issue to consider is the cultural value framework of Indonesia's multi-cultural society. Frank and straightforward reporting of controversial issues is valued highly in Western countries. In the context of Indonesia, such a reporting style might well be considered overly confrontational and, therefore, culturally inadequate. As one of the focus group participants aptly put it: "People in these countries might speak right to the point, but our people love beating around the bush."

Third, technology and access to advanced technical devices also set trainers and trainees apart in many cases. The trainers sometimes used sophisticated gadgets and equipment as part of the training, which made little sense as very few trainees had any access to such technology in their everyday work. In other words, international media training organizations have often failed to take into account the technology gap between Indonesia and the Western world.

Finally, as a number of focus group discussions show, there is a definite gap between the editorial side of radio news production and economic imperatives. More often than not, trainers concentrated exclusively on newsgathering routines and editorial processes. Such a narrow focus is mostly incompatible with the structural conditions in which most trainees have to operate. Except for a few journalists affiliated with the RRI public radio channel, the trainees generally work for privately owned radio channels funded by advertising alone. This reality tends to be ignored by Western trainers who often work for public service broadcasters such as the BBC or Deutsche Welle, where economic considerations are of lesser concern.

REFERENCES

Bollen, Kenneth, Pamela Paxton, and Rumi Morishima. 2005. "Assessing International Evaluations: An Example from USAID's Democracy and Governance Program." *American Journal of Evaluation* 26 (2): 189–203.

Edeani, David O. 1993. "Role of Development Journalism in Nigeria's Development." *Gazette* 52: 123–143.

Fair, Jo E. 1989. "29 Years of Theory and Research on Media and Development: The Dominant Paradigm Impact." *Gazette* 44: 129–150.

Gazali, Effendi. 2002. *Penyiaran Mutlak tapi Perlu*. Jakarta: Penerbit Jurusan Ilmu Komunikasi FISIP UI.

Golding, Peter. 1977. "Media Professionalism in the Third World: The Transfer of an Ideology." In *Mass Communication and Society*, edited by James Curran, Michael Gurevitch and Janet Woollacott, 291–308. London: Arnold.

Hakim, Catherine. 2000. *Research Design: Successful Designs for Social and Economic Research*. 2nd ed. New York: Routledge.

Hanitzsch, Thomas. 2005. "Journalists in Indonesia: Educated but Timid Watchdogs." *Journalism Studies* 6 (4): 493–508.

Hedebro, Goran. 1982. *Communications and Social Change in Developing Nations: A Critical View*. Ames: Iowa State University Press.

Jurriens, Edwin. 2007. "The Cosmopatriotism of Indonesia's Radio-active Public Sphere." *Thamyris/Intersecting: Place, Sex and Race* 16 (1): 105–132.

Kitley, Philip. 2000. *Television, Nation and Culture in Indonesia*. Athens: Ohio University.

Kumar, Krishna. 2006a. "International Assistance to Promote Independent Media in Transition and Post Conflict Societies." *Democratization* 13 (4): 652–667.

Kumar, Krishna. 2006b. *Promoting Independent Media: Strategic for Democracy Assistance*. Boulder, CO: Lynne Rienner Publishers.

LaMay, Craig. 2007. *Exporting Press Freedom: Economic and Editorial Dilemmas in International Media Assistance*. New Brunswick, NJ: Transaction Publishers.

Lindsay, Jennifer. 1997. "Making Waves: Private Radio and Local Identities in Indonesia". *Indonesia* 64 (Oct.): 105–123.

Muchtar, Nurhaya. 2010. "Understanding Management of International Media Training Overseas." *Communications Media Journal* 2 (1): 79–92.

Muchtar, Nurhaya, and Eric Haley. 2008. "Realities of Media Trainers Overseas: A Phenomenological Study." Paper presented at the Association of Journalism and Mass Communication (AEJMC), Chicago, August.

Napoli, James J. 2002. "International Journalism Education at the End of History, Starting in Albania." *Journalism and Mass Communication Educator* 57 (3): 260–270.

Peet, Richard, and Elaine Hartwick. 1999. *Theories of Development*. New York: The Guilford Press.

Pintak, Lawrence, and Budi Setiyono. 2011. "The Mission of Indonesian Journalism: Balancing Democracy, Development, and Islamic Values." *International Journal of Press/Politics* 16 (2): 185–209.

Richstad, Jim. 2000. "Asian Journalism in the Twentieth Century." *Journalism Studies* 1 (2): 273–284.

Rogers, Everett. 1971. *Diffusion of Innovation*. New York: The Free Press of Glencoe.

Rogers, Everett. 1976. "Communication and Development: The Passing of the Dominant Paradigm." *Communication Research* 3 (2): 213–240.

Romano, Angela. 2003. *Politics and the Press in Indonesia: Understanding an Evolving Political Culture*. New York: Routledge Curzon.

Romano, Angela. 2005. "Asian Journalism: News, Development and the Tides of Liberalization and Technology." In *Journalism and Democracy in Asia*, edited by Angela Romano and Michael Bromley, 1–14. London: Routledge.

Sen, Krishna. 2003. "Radio Days: Media-politics in Indonesia." *Pacific Review* 16 (4): 573–590.

Sen, Krishna, and David Hill. 2006. *Media, Culture and Politics in Indonesia*. Oxford: Oxford University Press.

Soeharto. 1989. "Role of the Press in National Development." In *Press Systems in ASEAN States*, edited by A Mehra, 131–134. Singapore: AMIC.

Soekomihardjo, Soetojo. 2003. "Radio Pemerintah: Antara Ada, Tiada, dan Haruskah Ada?" In *Cakram Komunikasi*, 39. Jakarta: Duta Cakrawala Komunika.

Susanto, Astrid. 1974. *The Mass Communication System in Indonesia*. Cambridge, MA: Center of International Studies, Massachusetts Institute of Technology.

Sussman, Gerald, and John A Lent. 1991. "Introduction: Critical Perspectives on Communication and Third World Development." In *Transnational Communication: Wiring the Third World*, edited by Gerald Sussman and John A Lent, 1–26. Newbury Park, CA: Sage.

Valentine, Sue. 2005. "When Journalism Training Isn't Enough". *Nieman Reports* 59 (2). http://www.nieman.harvard.edu/reports/article/101129/When-Journalism-Training-Isnt-Enough.aspx.

Wong, Kokkeong. 2004. "Asian-based Development Journalism and Political Elections: Press Coverage of the 1999 General Elections in Malaysia." *Gazette* 66: 25–40.

INVESTIGATIVE JOURNALISM ON CAMPUS
The Australian experience

Ian Richards and **Beate Josephi**

Despite many obstacles, investigative journalism continues to flourish in Australia. A significant part of the explanation for this appears to lie with universities which have journalism programs. Investigative journalism has a strong presence in these programs across Australia, a presence which is increasingly being felt at postgraduate level. As a result, an increasing number of journalism graduates have the skills and understanding necessary to embark on serious investigative work, and several institutions have embarked on projects with innovative approaches to collaborative investigative work. However, the wider context in which Australia's tertiary institutions operate is far from benign, and journalism programs—and thus the teaching of investigative journalism—are subject to many pressures. The paper finds that, although university journalism programs are increasingly taking responsibility for educating their students about investigative journalism, thereby picking up a key responsibility which would once have been borne entirely by the industry, there are also forces at work which limit their capacity to do this.

Introduction

This paper is as much about a mindset as it is about skills—that is the mindset of cherishing investigative journalism as the high art of journalism. As Matheson has pointed out, investigative journalism plays a major symbolic role because it represents journalism at its best and can be seen "often spectacularly, to be carrying out the fourth estate role described in the Anglo-American liberal tradition" (2010, 82). In Australia, investigative journalism is one of the forms which the Australian media consider to be their "best foot forward" to maintain readers, listeners and viewers (Josephi 2011, 33).

In many ways, questions about competency in journalism translate into establishing whether skills taught at tertiary institutions are adequate to meet the needs of the industry into which many graduates become immersed. What the needs of industry are, however, can be a vexed question. Different media have different requirements, and the same media frequently vary over time and place. Underlying these requirements is the issue of industry training, for the nature and extent of the responsibility of the industry for training new entrants has been an ongoing source of disputation, as have the role and responsibilities of universities in regard to the field of journalism.

However, the answers to competency questions have become more urgent over the past decade as technological advances have led to deep-reaching changes in the fundamental condition of journalism. The convergence of traditional and digital platforms has been compounded by shifts in the business model that has supported journalism for more than a century. The question with regard to skills therefore not only extends to asking whether students are conversant with new technologies but also whether they can adapt to new forms of information transmission as demanded by a dramatically changing social and economic environment.

Journalism in Western liberal democracies has long been defined as the Fourth Estate, meaning that the press provides essential checks and balances on government and business, and is as such an integral part of "an active and healthy body politic" (Zelizer 2005, 208). This interpretation of journalism's role has led to investigative journalism being regarded as the apex of journalism. Woodward and Bernstein's Watergate investigations are invariably cited as the pinnacle of what Hallin has described as the "high modernist" phase in American journalism (1994, 172). But with the "material conditions of contemporary journalism" (Phillips, Couldry, Freedman 2010, 51) being so substantially different from the 1970s, is investigative journalism still seen as the high art of journalism which, as Ettema and Glasser (1998, 1–15) have argued, elevates the reporters' craft to a moral discourse?

In Australia, the answer seems to be in the affirmative. Our argument for the continuing importance of investigative journalism in the Australian media and in Australian tertiary institutions rests on the following findings. In surveys of global journalists, Australia scores very high on questions relating to the importance of investigating government claims. Ninety percent of Australian journalists consider this to be "extremely important" (Josephi and Richards 2012, 121). This is 8 percent higher than in the previous survey, conducted 15 years earlier (Henningham 1998, 102; Weaver 1998, 446). Few other countries allocate such importance to the watchdog role. In 2002 in the United States, often seen as the paragon of investigative journalism, only 71 percent of journalists considered investigating government claims to be extremely important (Weaver et al. 2007, 140).

This result is underpinned by the fact that Australia's highest journalism prizes awarded by the industry to their peers, the Walkley Awards, have usually been won for investigative pieces (O'Donnell 2009). In 2011, tellingly, the prize for the "Most Outstanding Contribution to Journalism" was awarded to WikiLeaks. Although the decision was contentious, and was criticized in some quarters because the Australian editor-in-chief of Wikileaks, Julian Assange, is not a journalist, the citation appeared to acknowledge a significant act of investigative journalism when it stated that the winner "has shown a courageous and controversial commitment to the finest traditions of journalism: justice through transparency" and lauded Assange for taking "a brave, determined and independent stand for freedom of speech and transparency that has empowered people all over the world" (Walkley Foundation 2011).

Investigative journalism has a long pedigree in Australia. As long ago as the 1870s, journalist Henry Britton of the *Melbourne Argus* exposed the evils of blackbirding, the inhumane practice by which Pacific Islanders, generically referred to as "Kanakas", were forcibly recruited by unscrupulous sea captains and forced to work in Queensland's sugar plantations (Lloyd 2002, 13). Britton's approach was taken further in the 1880s through the work of Melbourne editor and journalist Maurice Brodzky, who investigated "the lawlessness, waste and commercial malpractice which ruined hundreds of investors" (Lloyd 2002, 13). The investigative tradition has been strengthened since that time through a host of successful investigations, from revelations of widespread institutional corruption in the state of Queensland in 1987 to exposes in 2012 of the conditions under which Australian livestock were being slaughtered in countries such as Indonesia and Pakistan.

Lloyd concluded that there were seven "investigative categories" relevant to Australian news history and journalistic practice—the journalist as watchdog; the journalist as agitator/crusader; the journalist and social responsibility/accountability; the journalist and the Fourth Estate; the journalist and the yellow press/muckraking; the journalist as explorer/fossicker; and the journalist as sleuth (2002, 5–12). These categories continue through to the present day, and are echoed in much of the current literature on Australian investigative journalism. Most Australian understandings of "investigative journalism" borrow from elsewhere. Thus the work of Briton Hugo de Burgh, for example, is widely referenced in Australia, as when Tom Morton (University of Technology, Sydney) approvingly quoted de Burgh's observation that, if journalism is the first rough draft of history, "by contrast, investigative journalism provides the first rough draft of legislation" (cited in Morton 2012, 13). For Morton, investigative journalism "may seek to expose injustice, hold the powerful to account, right wrongs, and give a voice to those who have no power and no influence; but ultimately the test of our work is whether it is able, directly or indirectly, to bring about change" (2012, 13–14).

The long tradition of exposure and revelation through investigative journalism, the survey results reported above, and the decision to award Assange as well as the citation, all attest to the high regard in which this form of journalism is held in Australia. The Australian context suggested the following research questions:

RQ1: Does the positioning of investigative journalism in journalism courses at Australian universities reflect the symbolic role played by investigative journalism in liberal democracies?

RQ2: What forces have contextualized the development of investigative journalism courses at Australian universities?

RQ3: How is investigative journalism incorporated into the curriculum of Australian universities?

RQ4: What activities/centres do universities have to support the pursuit of investigative journalism?

Our findings are based on a mainly qualitative analysis of investigative journalism in the Australian tertiary context.

What Competency?

A rich literature on competency has grown over the past decade (Bardoel and Deuze 2001; de Burgh 2003; Deuze, Bruns, and Neuberger 2007; MacMillan 2009; Opgenhaffen, Corten, and d'Haenens 2011; Iyer 2010). Much of this literature has addressed issues surrounding the impact of technological changes in the media on teaching and training, and the implications for student journalists. Part of the discussion has also been about the question of whether journalism education should, as Iyer (2010, 23) puts it, "be about imparting a set of skills or the preparation of a philosophical mind infused with the spirit of inquiry?" Iyer, who worked for the Australian national newspaper, *The Australian*, takes the industry position in which, somewhat inexplicably, an inquiring mind is seen as antithetical to acquiring skills needed for the journalistic profession. While it is clear that journalists require the practical abilities to perform the essential tasks of content production, an inquiring mind is precisely what leads to "the finest traditions of journalism" (Walkley Foundation 2011).

In recent years, Australian and New Zealand journalism academics have intensified their efforts to give investigative journalism greater prominence in their teaching and research. In December 2010, a conference on "Media, Investigative Journalism and Technology" was held at Auckland University of Technology. This was followed by the "Back to the Source" conference held by the University of Technology Sydney's Australian Centre for Independent Journalism (ACIJ) in September 2011, at which the Executive Director of the Centre for Investigative Reporting in Berkeley, California was a keynote speaker (ACIJ 2012).

When papers from the Auckland conference were published in the *Pacific Journalism Review* (vol. 17, no. 1), the editor and convenor of the first conference, Professor David Robie, highlighted the significance of investigative journalism:

> [I]t is a form of journalism that creates considerable benefits: it creates public transparency of powerful institutions and strengthens a publication's brand, arguably establishing a foundation where solutions to public interest issues can be explored. It also identifies relevance and purpose for the Fourth Estate as a profession. (2011, 5)

The contributions to the journal issue reveal that in tertiary institutions investigative journalism is seen in a variety of contexts, which range from strengthening future journalists' tools in dealing with sources (Hollings 2011) to exposing endemic corruption in Asian and Pacific Island states (Dixit 2011) to calls for a joint multimedia website, on which journalism students can publish their investigative pieces (Birnbauer 2011).

Australian Universities and Investigative Journalism

More than a decade ago, a national study of investigative journalism in Australia reported that there was widespread fear among the Australian journalistic community that investigative journalism was "dying, or at best foundering" (Haxton 2002, 33). The study, which included interviews with 23 investigative practitioners, concluded that Australian journalists were "in a life and death struggle to maintain the *raison d'être* of their profession, under sometimes incredible pressure" (Haxton 2002, 34). Since that time, Australia's media outlets have had to contend with the global financial crisis, the rise of social media, and the consolidation of media ownership. As newspapers, in particular, have come under great pressure, many journalists have been retrenched and employment levels across the industry have fallen and, as a result, support and resources for investigative journalism have become even more limited than it was at the time of Haxton's study.

Yet, despite the difficulties, there continue to be many successful investigative exposes by a growing list of print, radio, television and online journalists of everything from cases of wrongful imprisonment to the conditions under which Australian cattle were being slaughtered in Indonesian meatworks. The obvious question which arises is why, despite the many obstacles, investigative journalism continues to flourish in Australia.

Part of the explanation appears to lie with the personalities of those practitioners who are attracted to work as investigative journalists. In the United States, it has been claimed that investigative journalists bring considerable "dedication and zealotry" to their work which enables them to persist in the worst of times and "sometimes they seemingly flourish when the challenges are greatest" (Houston 2010, 47). A similar case could be made in Australia as there is little doubt that the country's investigative journalists are a tough and committed group of individuals.

However, a significant part of the explanation for the on-going success of investigative journalism appears to lie with universities which have journalism programs. In recent years in Australia, as elsewhere, there has been "a trend towards universities playing an increasingly central role in contributing to formations of journalistic professionalism" (Nolan 2008, 746). One of the consequences of this trend has been an opening up of what Nolan has described as "significant opportunities for forms of university education to act as an important check on some of the more deleterious effects engendered by the increased commercialization and deregulation of the media sector that has occurred in recent times" (747). As indicated above, one of these deleterious effects is shrinking resources to support investigative journalism. While the situation in Australia appears not to have declined to the extent experienced in the United Kingdom where, more than a decade ago, universities had "become essential in the transmission of the skills and public service values of investigative journalism" (Hanna 2008, 168), university-level journalism programs are increasingly assuming responsibility for training investigative journalists.

Universities with journalism programs are well suited to this role. According to Tom Fiedler of Boston University (quoted in Houston 2010, 49), American university assets include motivated students who can be trained to carry out much of the legwork that characterizes investigative journalism; staff who are experienced investigative journalists with the capacity to supervise and train these students; access to university resources that can assist investigations such as libraries, data bases, law faculty and a range of experts in such key fields such as finance, banking and accounting; and an administrative infrastructure that includes protection in terms of legal liability and insurance.

These points all translate smoothly to the Australian context. In addition, as indicated earlier, practice-based research has recently been boosted by the Federal Government's Excellence in Research for Australia (ERA) initiative, the stated aim of which is to "assess research quality within Australia's higher education institutions using a combination of indicators and expert review by committees comprising experienced, internationally-recognised experts" (Australian Research Council 2012). Significantly, the ERA process accommodates industry outputs from journalism academics provided they are of "quality", meaning that such outputs need to have a demonstrable and extensive research component if they are to count. As investigative journalism meets these criteria, it is not too long a bow to draw to conclude that an unintended consequence of the introduction of the ERA has been to encourage some journalism academics to undertake investigative journalism.

At the same time, however, it would be wrong to over-estimate the capacity of journalism staff and journalism students to undertake such investigations. While there is a growing group of practitioners who undertake university study in order to learn the techniques and methods of investigative journalism, most students are not working journalists. They are still "learning the ropes", and cannot be expected to perform the same role as an experienced practitioner. In addition, institutions have legal obligations to their students, not least what is known in Australia as a "duty of care", which means not putting students in situations—not uncommon in investigative journalism—in which they might come to physical or psychological harm.

In a wider sense, the environment in which Australia's universities operate is far from benign, and journalism programs regularly come under a range of internal and external pressures. Over the years these pressures have ranged from industry efforts to make course content compatible with the requirements of particular newsrooms to institutional pressures to increase student numbers. In the intensely competitive environment of the Australian tertiary sector, many institutions have moved to develop course content which distinguishes them from competing programs in the expectation that this will give them an advantage in an increasingly competitive market for students. Thus the University of Tasmania in Hobart, for example, has developed a strong focus on environmental journalism.

The capacity to pursue investigative journalism projects at Australian universities is further contextualized by Australia's research ethics requirements. Any research conducted which involves humans requires prior approval from a university ethics committee. Known as Human Research Ethics Committees, the composition and role of these committees is laid down in the *National Statement on Ethical Conduct in Human Research*, drawn up by the Australian Health Ethics Committee, a section of the National Health and Medical Research Council. Among the more contentious requirements for journalism academics seeking to undertake or encourage students to undertake investigative journalism are ethics requirements around such elements as interviewing, consent and deception (for fuller discussion, see for example, Richards 2009a). Obtaining ethics approval usually requires the applicant to work out questions weeks before the actual interview takes place, and to present them for formal approval, which is contrary to standard journalistic practice and antithetical to investigative journalism.

Informed consent can also be an issue. As one of the authors of this paper has argued elsewhere (Richards 2009a), seeking written consent can be problematic for journalists, who frequently interview individuals in powerful positions who are quite capable of agreeing or declining to be interviewed without requiring the formality of a consent form. Similarly, "it would be difficult to argue that consent should always be obtained from those who are crooked, corrupt or criminal prior to their actions being reported in the news media" (Richards 2009b, 18). Further difficulties for investigative projects can arise from the common requirement that participants in research should remain anonymous, and from the reluctance of most ethics committees to approve behaviour which deceives those under investigation. Even "respect for persons", the fundamental underlying principle of research ethics, poses difficulties, not least because if those being investigated are members of the Ku Klux Klan or the Nazi Party, for example, they "might merit humanity qualified with disapproval and . . . might on occasion appropriately be challenged aggressively in an interview" (Nelson 2004, 210).

Findings and Discussion

In 2012, 42 universities and colleges offered journalism programs in six of Australia's states and one of its two territories (Dunn 2012, 26). Most of these programs were located in public universities based in state capitals, although a small number were in universities based in smaller regional centres, including Bathurst and Wollongong in NSW, and Toowoomba and Townsville in Queensland. Some of the state universities also have regional campuses where journalism is taught, such as Deakin University's campus at

Warrnambool in western Victoria. There are also several private providers of journalism education, including Bond University on Queensland's Gold Coast, J-School in Brisbane and Macleay College in Sydney. All of the tertiary courses incorporate investigative journalism into their curricula, although the extent to which this occurs, and how, varies. Increasingly, investigative journalism is being taught at postgraduate rather than undergraduate level, generally as part of the coursework Masters programs which have developed at many universities over the past decade or so. This development has proved to be a particular benefit to journalism practitioners interested in developing their investigative skills and understanding. By allowing them to incorporate their professional experience and gain credit towards their studies, non-conventional doctorates and coursework Masters degrees provide "an avenue for established journalists who often lack opportunity in the workplace to build their knowledge and skills in critical and reflective forms of production" (interview, 2011). It has often been these people who then hand on their extensive experience as working journalists to students of journalism.

If it is the case that "a curriculum ebbs and flows continuously with the demands of life and the dictates of nature" (Bertelsen and Goodboy 2009, 271), then tertiary journalism curricula have ebbed and flowed a great deal in Australia. Since the first tertiary journalism program began at the University of Queensland in 1922, times of intense activity in curriculum development have been interspersed with extended periods of inactivity. Perhaps the most notable active period was from 1972 to 1975, under the Whitlam Labor Government, when many of Australia's current journalism programs were established. Most were located in what were then colleges of advanced education or institutes of technology, although these have long since been subsumed into the university system. For example, Curtin University in Perth was created in 1987 from the former Western Australian Institute of Technology, and Queensland University of Technology was formed from the amalgamation of the Queensland Institute of Technology and Brisbane College of Advanced Education.

What should be taught to the aspiring journalists who enrolled in these programs has been a subject of extended and often heated debate ever since. Key points of tension in this debate include the balance between the requirements of industry and the demands of academic enquiry; the place of theory and the place of practice; whether journalism is a craft or a profession; the relevance of non-journalism disciplines and the extent to which the fruits of these disciplines should be incorporated into curricula; and the deeper questions raised by the juxtaposition of journalistic models from the globe's industrialized "north" with those of the developing "south" (for fuller discussion, see for example, Hirst 2010; Josephi 2009).

Although the course content of the various programs which developed had much in common, there were also many variations, generally arising from a combination of the local set of circumstances in which particular programs were set up and the concerns of the practitioners who were initially recruited to staff these programs. Although this is not the place to discuss them in detail, all journalism programs have also been subjected to a range of pressures from governments, employers and students. Despite the difficulties they have faced, Australia's journalism programs have been remarkably successful in providing graduates for industry. In the most recent survey of Australian journalists conducted in 2010 (Josephi and Richards 2012), the overwhelming majority (84 percent) of Australian journalists had a university degree. Of those who completed an advanced degree in graduate or professional school, 61 percent did so in journalism or broadcast journalism, and a further 6 percent in communications. It is clear that today Australia's tertiary journalism programs play a key role in determining what aspects of journalism are taught, which journalistic forms are emphasized, and which nascent skills are taken by new entrants into the industry. Thus they also play a key role in shaping the nation's investigative journalism.

Content and Competencies

Perhaps the initial point to address is what is meant by the term "investigative journalism"? Ironically, some of investigative journalism's best-known practitioners have denied its very existence. Thus one of the foremost investigative journalists, Australian John Pilger, has argued that the term should be "rejected as a tautology since all journalists should be investigative" (quoted in de Burgh 2008, 13), while the late Paul Foot described investigative journalism as "a pretentious phrase without genuine meaning" (1999, 80). Yet, despite such attitudes, in Australia the term appears regularly in public and practitioner discourse, as well as in university course outlines, along with such titles as "investigative writing" and "investigative features". In other cases, investigative journalism is subsumed under the umbrella of "journalism research" and "statistics". But although there is some ambiguity in the way the term is defined, there is a commonality regarding its underlying purpose which is clearly encapsulated in Wendy Bacon's observation that teaching investigative journalism means "instilling in student journalists the understanding that journalism is about more than telling stories and passing on information—it's about finding information people don't know and turning it into stories" (interview, March 25, 2011).

Both generic and discipline-specific competencies are taught at all of the Australian universities with journalism programs. The former are primarily in the form of a set of general skills required of all graduates regardless of disciplinary background. For example, the University of South Australia (2012) lists seven "graduate qualities" expected of the university's graduates; these cover everything from problem solving to the ability to communicate and acquire international perspectives. But although these qualities all have general relevance to the practice of investigative journalism, what is taught under its specific banner is far more significant.

Journalism education in universities is normally organized around three curricular axes or lines of development (UNESCO 2007). These are an axis comprising the norms, values, tools, standards and practices of journalism; an axis emphasizing the social, cultural, political, economic, legal and ethical aspects of journalism practice both within and outside national borders; and an axis comprising knowledge of the world and journalism's intellectual challenges (UNESCO 2007, 6–7). The three axes meet in the study of the role and practice of investigative journalism, for investigative courses invariably build on a foundation of knowledge of journalism acquired in prerequisite courses in which students acquire understanding of the norms, values, tools, standards and practices of journalism; the social, cultural, political, economic, legal and ethical aspects of journalism practice; and the place of journalism in the world and journalism's intellectual challenges. Examples of course content include reporting, writing, ethics and the role of journalism in a liberal democracy as well as a range of practical workshops which, in effect, aim to teach students how to become an investigative journalist. In other words, one strand of study focuses on investigative research techniques and the other focuses on developing an understanding of the role of investigative journalism and the "public right to know" in a democratic society. In this way, knowledge of the context of investigative journalism and its social significance augments a range of practical competencies including practical research techniques, problem-solving, the use of public records and documents, use of databases and the legal framework within which investigations can take place.

In all of Australia's journalism programs, investigative journalism is presented as the pinnacle of journalistic achievement. This can be explained by the fact that the overwhelming majority of Australia's journalism academics began their careers as practitioners and so share the wider professional perception that investigative journalism most closely embodies the traditional Fourth Estate role of the press. At the time of writing, seven universities have investigative journalism in name as a subject[1] in their journalism courses. Most of these are offered at both undergraduate and postgraduate level, and two only at postgraduate level. Other universities include elements of investigative journalism in subjects such as political or environmental journalism.

At a practical level, a growing number of Australian programs have built on this common understanding to develop collaborative investigative projects using students and staff from a number of institutions. Overseen by experienced journalism practitioners, students undertake investigative projects, which—provided they meet appropriate standards—can subsequently be published. A notable example of this is provided by the decision of a number of universities in Australia, New Zealand and the Pacific region to form a network in which students studying investigative or in-depth reporting complete assignments on similarly themed issues. Under the proposal, "the best work would be augmented by editing, videos, and graphics and posted on a website tentatively called UniMuckraker, providing a national or regional perspective of a significant issue" (Birnbauer 2011). According to its originator, Bill Birnbauer of Monash University, teaching with "real journalism" provides "an authentic, contextual and team-oriented approach to higher education learning while offering a broader audience a new outlet for quality journalism with concurrent additional opportunities for publication in mainstream media" (interview, 2011). The UniMuckraker project draws on US models where a number of producers of investigative journalism have used tertiary students either as interns, research assistants, reporters, assistant editors or video producers. As an example, Birnbauer suggests the International Consortium of Investigative Journalists, a project of the investigative reporting non-profit organization, the Centre for Public Integrity, under which investigative reporters in many parts of the world work collaboratively on stories that transcend borders (interview, May 5, 2011).

A second model is provided by the ACIJ at the University of Technology, Sydney. ACIJ runs three to four classes on investigative journalism each year for undergraduates, offers a Graduate Certificate in Investigative Journalism and a MA in Journalism that includes an investigative journalism unit (ACIJ 2012). With the guidance of staff, ACIJ students produce journalism, especially investigative journalism, and also work with freelance journalists, academics and industry, with the work being published online (ACIJ 2012). Wendy Bacon, former Professor of Journalism based at the ACIJ, says that the underlying philosophy is to support independent journalism via a range of activities "from research to investigative projects" (interview, March 25, 2011). She says there is much greater interest today than there once was in new forms of independent journalism and new funding models. Bacon has previously made clear her view that investigative journalism projects involving students conducted through university-based journalism programs are in the public interest and underscore "the public service goals of journalism and universities" (2011, 63). Investigative projects conducted by ACIJ in recent years include a study on the quality of Australian media reporting on climate change; an investigation of the conditions suffered by people with mental illness in public housing in the western suburbs of Sydney; and a comparison of the coverage by Australia's national daily newspapers of the *News of the World* hacking story as "an ideal litmus test of the independence of the 70% of Australian newspaper journalists employed in the Murdoch stable" (ACIJ 2012). Several other universities have shown interest in this model, and it seems likely that more centres with the capacity to undertake investigative journalism will be established in the near future.

Both the ACIJ and Monash programs have benefited from the employment of staff who have many years' experience as investigative journalists and whose work has been published across the Australian media. This is not the case at all institutions, a situation which appears to have inhibited the development of investigative ventures at some other campuses. However, while as yet few other universities have centres like the ACIJ, all universities with journalism programs encourage student journalism to publication, and some of this output is investigative in nature.

Conclusion

From the preceding discussion, it can be seen that investigative journalism has a strong presence in tertiary journalism programs across Australia, a presence which is increasingly being felt at postgraduate level. Although this presence is demonstrated in different ways, across the country course curricula incorporate practical and theoretical aspects of investigative journalism, in the process combining the teaching of investigative research techniques with the development of an understanding of the role of investigative journalism and the "public right to know" in a democratic society. In many ways, these investigative journalism courses embody the meeting point of the three curricular axes of journalism education (UNESCO 2005)—an axis comprising the norms, values, tools, standards and practices of journalism; an axis emphasizing the social, cultural, political, economic, legal and ethical aspects of journalism practice both within and outside national borders; and an axis comprising knowledge of the world and journalism's intellectual challenges.

One consequence of this situation is that an increasing number of journalism students are graduating with the skills and understandings necessary to embark on serious investigative work. This is particularly beneficial for those graduates who are able to operate in an environment where such activity is supported and encouraged. However, not all employers support such activity, especially when it is undertaken by recent graduates, and independent investigations are difficult to carry out. This underlines the significance of investigative projects at those institutions with innovative approaches to collaborative investigative work.

It is important to remember that the wider context in which Australia's journalism programs operate is far from benign, and the teaching of journalism—in common with other disciplines—is subject to many pressures. Investigative journalism is not immune from these pressures. Although, on one hand, investigative journalism on campus appears to have been given an unintended boost by the recognition of practice-based research by the Federal Government's ERA initiative, on the other hand investigative journalism on campus is subject to many factors which impede its development. These range from the legal and ethical requirements of universities to the resourcing issues being experienced across the entire tertiary sector. Perhaps the most basic restriction is simply that most students are not working journalists, and thus cannot be expected to perform the same role as experienced investigators.

In summary, then, university journalism programs in Australia are increasingly taking responsibility for educating their students about investigative journalism, thereby picking up a key responsibility which would once have been borne entirely by the industry. At the same time, however, there are forces at work which limit their capacity to do this. The situation appears to justify qualified optimism, although what will happen in the longer term remains an unknown quantity.

NOTE

1. The designation of awards and courses in Australia varies from university to university. The components of a three-year journalism undergraduate degree normally consist of four subjects or units being studied per semester. The same applies to the normally two-year postgraduate degree.

REFERENCES

ACIJ (Australian Centre for Independent Journalism). 2012. "Australian Centre for Independent Journalism." Accessed March 30. http://acij.uts.edu.au/.

Australian Research Council. 2012. "The Excellence in Research for Australia (ERA) Initiative." Accessed April 4. http://www.arc.gov.au/era/default.htm.

Bacon, Wendy. 2011. "Investigative Journalism in the Academy—Possibilities for Storytelling across Time and Space." *Pacific Journalism Review* 17 (1): 45–66.

Bardoel, Jo, and Mark Deuze. 2001. "'Network Journalism': Converging Competencies of Old and New Media Professionals." *Australian Journalism Review* 23 (2): 91–103.

Bertelsen, Dale, and Alan Goodboy. 2009. "Curriculum Planning: Trends In Communication Studies, Workplace Competencies, and Current Programs at 4-Year Colleges and Universities." *Communication Education* 58 (2): 262–275.

Birnbauer, Bill. 2011. "Student Muckrakers: Applying Lessons from Non-profit Investigative Reporting in the US." *Pacific Journalism Review* 17 (1): 26–44.

de Burgh, Hugo. 2003. "Skills Are Not Enough: The Case for Journalism As an Academic Discipline." *Journalism* 4 (1): 95–112.

de Burgh, Hugo, ed., 2008. *Investigative Journalism: Context and Practice.* 2nd ed. London: Routledge.

Deuze, Mark, Axel Bruns, and Christoph Neuberger. 2007. "Preparing for an Age of Participatory News." *Journalism Practice* 1 (3): 322–338.

Dixit, Kunda. 2011. "Real Investigative Journalism in a Virtual World." *Pacific Journalism Review* 17 (1): 11–19.

Dunn, Anne. 2012. "Australia's Many Options for Studying Journalism." *Media Art and Design* March: 26–27.

Ettema, James S., and Theodore L. Glasser. 1998. *Custodians of Conscience—Investigative Journalism and Public Virtue*. New York: Columbia University Press.

Foot, Paul. 1999. "The Slow Death of Investigative Journalism." In *The Penguin Book of Journalism*, edited by Stephen Glover, 79–89. London: Penguin Books.

Hallin, Daniel. 1994. *We Keep America on Top of the World*. London: Routledge.

Hanna, Mark. 2008. "Universities as Evangelists of the Watchdog Role: Teaching Investigative Journalism to Undergraduates." In *Investigative Journalism*. 2nd ed., edited by Hugo de Burgh, 157–163. London: Routledge.

Haxton, Nance. 2002. "The Death of Investigative Journalism." In *Journalism Investigation and Research*, edited by Stephen Tanner, 20–36. Sydney: Longman-Pearson.

Henningham, John. 1998. "Australian Journalists." In *The Global Journalist—News People around the World*, edited by David Weaver, 91–107. Cresskill, NJ: Hampton Press.

Hirst, Martin. 2010. "Journalism Education 'Down Under': A Tale of Two Paradigms." *Journalism Studies* 11 (1): 83–98.

Hollings, James. 2011. "The Informed Commitment Model: Best Practice for Journalists Engaging with Reluctant, Vulnerable Sources and Whistle-blowers." *Pacific Journalism Review* 17 (1): 76–89.

Houston, Brant. 2010. "The Future of Investigative Journalism." *Daedalus* 139 (2): 45–56.

Iyer, Padma. 2010. "The Intellectual Component in Best Practices of Journalism." *Australia Pacific Media Educator* 20 (3): 23–31.

Josephi, Beate. 2009. "Journalism Education." In *The Handbook of Journalism Studies*, edited by Karin Wahl-Jorgensen and Thomas Hanitzsch, 42–56. London: Routledge.

Josephi, Beate. 2011. "Supporting Democracy: How Well Do the Australian Media Perform?" *Australian Journalism Monographs* 13: 6–46.

Josephi, Beate, and Ian Richards. 2012. "The Australian Journalist in the 21st Century." In *The Global Journalist in the 21st Century*, edited by David Weaver and Lars Willnatt, 115–125. London: Routledge.

Lloyd, Clem. 2002. "The Historical Roots." In *Journalism Investigation and Research*, edited by Stephen Tanner, 2–19. Frenchs Forest: Pearson.

MacMillan, Margie. 2009. "Watching Learning Happen: Results of a Longitudinal Study of Journalism Students." *Journal of Academic Librarianship* 35 (2): 132–142.

Matheson, Donald. 2010. "The Watchdog's New Bark: Changing Forms of Investigative Reporting." In *The Routledge Companion to News and Journalism*, edited by Stuart Allen, 82–92. London: Routledge.

Morton, Tom. 2012. "This Wheel's on Fire: New Models for Investigative Journalism." *Pacific Journalism Review* 18 (1): 13–16.

Nelson, Carey. 2004. "The Brave New World of Research Surveillance." *Qualitative Inquiry* 10 (2): 207–218.

Nolan, David. 2008. "Journalism, Education and the Formation of 'Public Subjects,'' *Journalism* 9 (6): 733–749.

O'Donnell, Penny. 2009. "That's Gold! Thinking about Excellence in Australian Journalism." *Australian Journalism Review* 39 (1): 47–60.

Opgenhaffen, Michael, Maarten Corten, and Leen d'Haenens. 2011. *Nieuwsvaardig. Een crossmediale competentiematrix voor journalisten* [Fit for News: A Crossmedia Competency Matrix for Journalists]. Leuven: Lannoo Campus.

Phillips, Angela, Nick Couldry, and Des Freedman. 2010. "An Ethical Deficit? Accountability, Norms, and the Material Conditions of Contemporary Journalism." In *New Media, Old*

News—Journalism and Democracy in the Digital Age, edited by Natalie Fenton, 51–67. London: Sage.

Richards, Ian. 2009a. "Uneasy Bedfellows: Ethics Committees and Journalism Research." *Australian Journalism Review* 31 (2): 35–46.

Richards, Ian. 2009b. "Managing the Margins: How Journalism Reports the Vulnerable." *Asia Pacific Media Educator* 19 (1): 15–22.

Robie, David. 2011. "Editorial: Reinventing Muckraking." *Pacific Journalism Review* 17 (1): 5–9.

UNESCO. 2007. *Model Curricula for Journalism Education in Developing Countries and Emerging Democracies*. Paris: UNESCO.

University of South Australia. 2012. "Graduate Qualities." Accessed April 14. http://www.unisa.edu.au/gradquals/default.asp.

Walkley Foundation. 2011. "The Walkley Foundation—2011 Award Winners." http://www.walkleys.com/2011winners#most-outstanding-contribution-to-journalism.

Weaver, David H. 1998. "Journalists around the World: Commonalities and Differences." In *The Global Journalist—News People around the World*, edited by David Weaver, 455–480. Cresskill, NJ: Hampton Press.

Weaver, David H., Randal A. Beam, Bonnie J. Brownlee, Paul S. Voakes, and Cleveland G. Wilhoit. 2007. *The American Journalist in the 21st Century: U.S. News People at the Dawn of a New Millennium*. Mahwah, NJ: Lawrence Erlbaum.

Zelizer, Barbie. 2005. "The Culture of Journalism." In *Mass Media and Society*, edited by James Curran and Michael Gurevitch, 198–214. London: Arnold.

BEYOND SKILLS TRAINING

Six macro themes in South African journalism education

Pieter J. Fourie

This article identifies and discusses six underlying socio-cultural and political themes in South African journalism education. The themes are apartheid and race, gender, development, freedom of expression, indigenization and the impact of the new media on journalism. The argument is that although South African journalism education is skills and career-oriented, the treatment of the themes and the issues related to them form the theoretical and intellectual foundation of South African journalism education. The underlying, theoretical point of departure is that journalism is a representation of reality or an aspect thereof. As such, journalism reflects society, which in the case of South Africa is a dichotomous one. South African journalism education is embedded in this society.

Introduction

In earlier and related work (Fourie 2005, 2010a, 2010b, 2011, 2012b) I expressed my concern about the domination of professional skills training in South African journalism education[1] and argued that a focus on such skills is to the detriment of the development of theoretical and intellectual skills and journalism research. I argued that the teaching of journalism skills identified as professional needs in two studies commissioned by the South African National Editors' Forum (Sanef) in 2002 and 2005 and by the South African Human Rights Commission in 2000 are predominant in South African journalism education. These studies give great importance to writing skills, interviewing skills, professional codes of conduct and, generally speaking, the acquisition of the "tricks of the trade".

In this article it is argued that although South African journalism education can still be characterized as being skills driven, six major socio-cultural and political themes embedded in the South African society and in the sociology of South African mediated communication (and dealt with in depth in Fourie 2010a, 2010b, 2011 and 2012b) can be seen as forming the theoretical and intellectual foundation of South African journalism education.

The purpose here is to describe how these themes and the issues they initiate guide South African journalism education. The themes are apartheid and race, gender, development, freedom of expression, indigenization, and the impact of the new media on journalism as a cultural product.

Methodologically the article is descriptive. The theoretical point of departure is representation theory[2] (see e.g. Downing and Husband 2005, 1–25). A view of journalism as representation underlies an emphasis in education on how journalism portrays and/or could portray the South African society, its citizens, politics and cultures.

The focus on macro themes and influences comes from Terzis's (2009)[3] overview of European journalism, in which it is argued that two macro developments or revolutionizing transformations dominate the nature and direction of European journalism education. That is (1) the political transformations which have taken place in the past two decades and (2) the development of information and communication technology (ICT). The first change has led, *inter alia*, to increased Democracy, or at least an almost worldwide push for more Democracy. As far as journalism is concerned, it has led to an increased acknowledgement of the importance of a free media and freedom of expression. The second change—ICT—has been contributing to globalization, convergence and digitization, three factors having widespread effects on the phenomenological nature of mass communication (and journalism), and leading to what is generally referred to as the changed media landscape. In different contributions from various countries, the researchers in Terzis's book show that these transformations cannot be disregarded as they form the backdrop in which journalism takes place and are the impetus for the nature of and the rethinking of the nature, value and future of journalism training and education.

Similarly, the democratization of South African society and the attendant liberalization of media regulations have impacted on South African journalism education. In the new society there is a greater sensitivity about race and identity and the devastating impact of racial discrimination on a society. With this, and in the context of social, cultural, educational, economic and political change, a new awareness of identity and a drive to protect and rediscover cultural identity have emerged. New media technology has given rise to a new media environment in South Africa, characterized by, *inter alia*, digitization, convergence and multimedia platforms and approaches. This has created an almost entirely new media and social culture. All of this has had an impact on journalism education, as will be described in this article.

When approaching journalism as representation, it can be argued that key questions such as the following underlie South African journalism education: What does South African journalism tell us about South African society? How is South African society represented in or communicated through journalism?

Theme One: Apartheid and Race

Almost two decades after its formal demise, apartheid continues to recur as a theme in South African social, cultural, political and economic practices. Time and again, apartheid and racism are blamed as the key cause of poverty, lack of development, poor education, poor services, poor government, conflict, and a continuing tendency towards racist and biased (stereotyped) representations of black people in cultural expressions, including in a "Western-biased" media and journalism.[4]

Apartheid practices and apartheid ideology have had an undeniable impact on South African journalism education. One can claim that the history of South African journalism and journalism education is a history of the representation of apartheid. This relationship between journalism education and apartheid is expounded by several South African researchers such as Banda et al. (2007), Berger (1998, 2007), De Beer (2000, 2008), Fourie (2002, 2007, 2009, 2010a, 2010b, 2012a), Prinsloo (2010), Steenveld (2007, 2008),

Teer-Tomaselli and Tomaselli (2001), Tomaselli and Caldwell (2002), Tomaselli (2000, 2009), Wasserman (2005a, 2005b, 2006a, 2006b), and Wasserman and De Beer (2004).

In various ways these authors deal with the impact of apartheid (and colonialism) on journalism, journalism education and "apartheid journalism" as such. In addition to the *us–them* dichotomy in South African journalism, this includes *the treatment of* racial issues from a perspective of inclusion/exclusion, and stereotypical understandings and representations of race.

De Beer (2008) argues that most work on South African journalism education has been conducted within the confines of higher education under apartheid and thereafter as part or against the struggle against apartheid. He classifies journalism education approaches into a number of paradigms based on their political positions and relationship(s) with the apartheid government, which, according to him, determined the schools' or departments' approaches to education and syllabi. The more conservative Afrikaans institutions used to be less critical of the apartheid government. The more liberal institutions, which supported the struggle against apartheid, were more critically oriented. Both concentrated mainly on journalistic skills. Today all are changing in various respects: language of tuition (becoming mostly English), achieving a student and staff population that is representative of the country's demographics (affirmative action), adopting an African perspective on journalism and the media (indigenization), etc.

According to De Beer, the "long-standing ideological schisms" between different educational institutions have made it difficult to achieve a coherent journalism education platform. He argues that only now are these divisions beginning to disappear (De Beer 2008, 191).

South African journalism education remains strongly influenced by two landmark studies on the impact of apartheid on journalism (specifically the racial and racist content of journalism) and the need for skills and management training. The two studies are: the South African Human Rights Commission's study on the South African media and race (SAHRC 2000), and the commissioned skills audits of Sanef (Steyn and De Beer 2002; Steyn, De Beer, and Steyn 2005).

These studies were motivated by what Sparks (2009, 15) calls Nelson Mandela's "concerns about the ethical limitations" of journalists in news offices, even before he took up the Presidency. This concern continued throughout Thabo Mbeki's term of office. Mbeki, however, focused on the lack of black media ownership as well as regulation, the limited number of black journalists in newsrooms, and the need for African journalistic perspectives on Africa and the world. These concerns continue under the presidency of Jacob Zuma. The emphasis now, however, is less on *Africanism* and more on a need to protect the government from so-called "Western-prejudiced journalism", which is often seen as one of the last cultural remnants of Western colonialism.

With several content analyses, the SAHRC study concluded that the South African media (with some exceptions) were inherently racist during apartheid, in terms of both content and practices. This finding led, among other things, to media houses and regulatory bodies and associations adopting new codes of conduct on how to deal with race and racial issues. See in this regard the codes of conduct of the Broadcasting Complaints Commission of South Africa (BCCSA, http://www.bccsa.co.za), the South African Press Code of the Press Ombudsman of the Press Council of South Africa (http://www.presscouncil.org.za) and Sanef (http://www.sanef.org.za).

Sanef's 2002 South African National Journalism Skills Audit revealed such shortcomings as a lack of accuracy in reporting, poor interviewing and research skills, and a general lack of language skills. It also emphasized the need for South African journalists and students to acquire a third language (preferably an African one), and pointed to a lack of conceptual skills—mostly poor analytical skills and general knowledge (including a deficient reading culture). The audit also highlighted the need for training in communication skills, motivational skills, professionalism and media law. These skills are still the focal point in South African journalism education.

The audit also mentioned the need for an improvement in management style (a move away from top-down management), news management (the need to develop news policies which are transparent and easy to implement), and the management of human resources, including issues such as affirmative action, mentoring, peer input, etc. The audit made a number of specific recommendations related to, among other things, improvement of reporting, writing and accuracy skills, improved interaction between the media industry and tertiary institutions, internships, and "training the trainers" (Steyn and De Beer 2002). Throughout, the report is sensitive to race and racial issues.

The second audit (Steyn, De Beer, and Steyn 2005) found that first-line managers in South African newsrooms were mostly male, young, had good educational credentials and were mostly English speakers. However, almost half of them seemed to be inexperienced in management. Specific needs included acquiring managerial skills, communication skills, teamwork skills and strategic planning skills. Many such skills are still lacking according to the more contemporary 2010 study of the National Press Club (Consulta 2010).

In short, the two landmark studies have led to syllabi placing an increased focus on the discriminatory and dehumanizing ways in which the apartheid media represented black people and people of color (see e.g. Steenveld 2008; *Ecquid Novi: African Journalism Education*, vol. 21, no. 2, 2000; *Rhodes Journalism Review*, May 14, 1997). Education emphasizes the need for future journalists to show sensitivity in their representations of race and gender. In addition, discriminatory employment policies in the media industry and racially skewed media ownership are underlined. Attention is also drawn to the racially and gender-skewed education policies of the past as well as the necessary changes.

Concerning regulation and the media, education focuses on racial equity and transformation in the media industry and thus on ways to undo inequities and racial injustices in media ownership, employment and access to the media.

However, despite journalism education's emphasis on racial equity and the reporting of racially loaded issues, the *us* versus *them* dichotomy is ever present in the South African media. Being a mirror of society, they reflect persistent—or even escalating—racist traits, prompting a prominent black journalist to write that

> we should be very afraid of the spectre of racial discourse that is reasserting itself in our national life [as reported in the media], as is happening now. Be it in the form of increasingly re-emerging white racism or in pockets of African chauvinism, it is something that can easily throw us back two decades. (Makhanya 2009, 12)

It is this racist discourse and the related questions of identity which receive considerable attention in journalism education and which raise considerable debate in journalism education, often of a high theoretical standard. (Also see the discussion of "The Spear" later.)

Theme Two: Gender, Equality and Stereotyping

The end of apartheid brought an end to discriminatory laws and, at least on paper, to the unequal and discriminatory treatment of people, not only in terms of race, but also gender, religion and sexual orientation.[5] Several laws are in place which support affirmative action in an attempt to create equity in South African society. In journalism education it has meant the appointment of greater numbers of Black, Coloured and Indian lecturers as well as administrative and production staff, and an increase in Black, Coloured and Indian students. Apart from race, there is also an emphasis on gender and the position of women in the media (both in reporting and employment policies and practices).

In 2003 Sanef committed to facilitating processes aimed at fostering diversity in the South African media. One of the outcomes was a research project under the title *The Glass Ceiling and beyond—The Status of Women and Diversity in the South African News Media*. The research was done in two phases (Sanef 2003, 2007). Glass Ceiling One found that despite having a Constitution which entrenches equal rights, "discriminatory practices, structural inequalities, cultural factors, prejudices, patriarchy and sexism still exist in South African newsrooms" (Sanef 2003).

In 2007, however, it was found that there were nearly equal numbers of women and men in newsrooms, with 45 percent women in newsrooms compared to 33 percent in a 1995 study. When it came to race, there was still a major discrepancy, with black women (46 percent of the population) only accounting for 18 percent of newsroom staff and black men (45 percent of the population) only accounting for 28 percent, compared to 28 percent white men—although the latter only made up 4 percent of the population.

The study also found that few women were in managerial positions in journalism, with less than 30 percent of women in top management positions (one in three senior managers in newsrooms). Conversely, they made up 48 percent of junior managers and almost 70 percent of all semi-skilled workers in the newsroom.

Concerning black males in managerial positions, the study found that there had been deliberate efforts to redress the racial imbalances of the past, with black men in top and senior positions rising from 16 percent in 1999 to 23.5 percent in 2006.

The executive summary of the second phase of Glass Ceiling (Sanef 2007) highlighted the following:

- Newsrooms with a higher proportion of women in decision-making positions also have higher levels of gender parity among the overall staff.
- Men are more likely than women to be employed in open-ended full-time contracts while women are more likely to be contracted on a part-time basis.
- Men earn more on average than women. While the income differential between white men and black men in newsrooms is narrowing, black women earn, on average, 25 percent less than white men in newsrooms.
- While there are now roughly equal proportions of women and men in the editorial divisions of newsrooms, women dominate the presenter and administrative categories while men make up the biggest percentage of the technical category.
- Male journalists dominate beats such as politics, economics, investigative reporting and crime. They also constitute over 90 percent of sports reporters. The only fields in which women journalists predominate are entertainment, education and general reporting.

The purpose of the above is to show how gender, and specifically the position of women, is a critical theme in South African society, with the media and journalism often taking the lead in continued efforts to correct the inequities of the past. Although complete parity (or proportionality) is still not achieved, there is nevertheless a heightened attentiveness to the position of women in the media and journalism industry.

As far as reporting and the content and practice of journalism are concerned, most media organizations have clear guidelines in their codes of conduct on how to deal with women and women's issues—which is of particular importance in a country where 66,196 sexual offenses (mainly rape) were committed in 2010/2011 (South African Police Service 2012). In journalism education, sensitivity about the reporting of women is consequently sharpened. There is also a heightened awareness of the negative effects of the stereotyped portrayal of gays, religious and minority ethnic groups. Making students aware of the nature, origin and working of stereotypes in journalism and of the negative effects of the representation thereof on people, culture and organizations is one of the main skills being dealt with in education.

Theme Three: Development Communication

A third macro theme is development. The emphasis on this theme can also be attributed to apartheid and the legacy of unequal development it has left behind. The theme is mainly dealt with in terms of the role of journalism in development, how journalism can serve people in local communities (at grassroots level), and how journalism can articulate citizens' views, needs and interests and communicate them to local, regional and national levels of government.

Considerable emphasis is placed on the question of access, not only in terms of creating access for the population to media, but also access in terms of media ownership and media literacy (how to produce and use the media and journalism for development purposes). (See in this regard the work of the Media Development and Diversity Agency, http://www.mdda.org.za.)

A crucial point in development is the disparity between the modernized, "elite" sector of the population and those still existing in poverty, and the effects thereof on access to and the use of the media (including the internet)—the "digital divide".

Increasing attention is also paid to the "new development paradigm" which is emerging from within Africa, and how such a paradigm affects or may eventually affect thinking about journalism and development. See in this regard the work of Ansu-Kyeremeh ([1997] 2005). In his and related work (see e.g. Morrison 2005, 16), it is emphasized that should journalism wish to contribute to development, then it should take cognizance of the (cultural) characteristics of African communication, such as

- acknowledging the importance of the symbolic power of language;
- the need for communication to express emotion, mood and atmosphere;
- the multimodal nature of African communication (including singing, dance, drama, storytelling, rhetorical speaking, the effective use of proverbs);
- acknowledging that communication (and especially mediated communication and journalism) should have a didactic function;
- the need for all public (mediated) communication to express community values;

- the need for public communication to comply with the demands of the art of rhythmic discussion "palaver" (chatter/gossip);
- acknowledging that African styles of communication are not just incidental, but incorporate fundamental cultural values. (Also see White 2008.)

The study of the characteristics of African communication and its application to journalism is a growing field and it can develop into a distinctive African focal point in journalism education (also see the discussion of indigenization).

To summarize: the emphasis on race, gender and development shows that South African journalism and journalism education cannot be disconnected from the influences of apartheid, also on the South African society at large. At the same time it demonstrates South African society and South African journalism's hyper-awareness of and concern—one might say obsession—with issues of race, gender, inequality, bias and discrimination, and how these are represented in journalism.

Theme Four: Democracy and Freedom of Expression

Under apartheid the media were severely censored and restricted (Fourie 2002, 2009). After the demise of apartheid, new liberalized forms of media legislation and regulation were adopted and freedom of expression was embedded in the Constitution. These developments were preceded with a well-documented struggle both inside and outside South Africa against media censorship and the right to freedom of expression. Soon after the first democratic election of a majority government (led by the African National Congress (ANC)) in 1994, the government introduced new media ownership legislation, statutory forms of regulation (see e.g. the Independent Communication Authority of South Africa (Icasa)) and institutionalized self-regulation (see e.g. BCCSA and the Press Ombudsman of the Press Council).

Despite these measures, the relationship between the media and the government started to grow tense soon after 1994, and it remains so today with ongoing attempts to curb the media and interfere with its independence (see Fourie 2009; the special edition on freedom of expression of the Afrikaans journal *Tydskrif vir Geesteswetenskappe*, vol. 49, March 2009); Milo's 2010 overview of threats to the media under the title "Chilly Winds Are Blowing around South African Media"; and Reid (2012) on regulation against the background of the 2012 fall in South Africa's international media freedom rating).

Freedom of expression, what it is, its relationship to Democracy, threats to it, how views about freedom of expression relate to ideology, and how freedom of expression can be indigenized are thus dealt with incessantly in South African journalism education (see e.g. the 2000–2012 editions of *Rhodes Journalism Review*, *Ecquid Novi: African Journalism Education* and *Communicatio: South African Journal for Communication Theory and Research*).

The government's intimidating treatment of the media and freedom of expression is illustrated by their attacks on the media for being "anti-government", "non-patriotic" and "unhelpful for national development". The following are some examples.

At its 2007 Polokwane Conference, the ANC government threatened to establish a Media Appeals Tribunal (MAT), a kind of disciplinary body meant to deal with complaints against the media—including many from the ANC. In a discussion document entitled "Communications and the Battle of Ideas", 26 points pertained to the media, including the introduction or establishment of MAT. Since 2007 the proposed tribunal has been hanging like a sword over the media and it is again on the agenda of the ANC conference in December 2012. Proposals call for it to be instituted in addition to existing self-regulatory institutions such as the BCCSA, Sanef and the office of the Press Ombudsman of the Press Council.

In June 2011, considering the ANC's threats, Print Media South Africa (PMSA) and Sanef took it upon themselves to create a Press Freedom Commission (PFC) meant to investigate the self-regulation of the print media, and especially the functioning of the Press Ombudsman. This was seen by many as an attempt by the print media to pre-empt the government's threat to set up a tribunal. In 2012, the PFC proposed reforms to the current print media regulation system that would, among other things, grant more rights and make it easier for members of the public to file complaints against the press.[6]

Nothing, though, caused more concern than the proposed Protection of State Information Bill. This Bill has been on the table for a number of years and has been referred back to committees a number of times. The Bill contains clauses which are, in terms of the Constitution, a serious threat not only to the media, but to the right to information of each and every citizen. Initially the Bill made it a punishable offence (up to 25 years in prison) for a journalist to possess, communicate or publish "classified" state information. It defined any government information as classifiable if it was seen by a politician and/or a civil servant to be harmful to the "national interest". The Bill was passed by the National Assembly in 2011, awaiting the approval of the National Council of Provinces and the President's signature. Under tremendous political and public pressure,[7] the government backed down in May 2012 and made some concessions to "soften" the Bill. At the time of writing (June 2012) the Bill was still not finalized.

A recent example of the government's interference and efforts to curb freedom of expression and lately also artistic expression is the case of "The Spear". This case will become an exemplary case study in South African journalism education about the balance between respecting human dignity, public interest, stereotyping race, freedom of expression and regulation, including internet and social media regulation.

"The Spear" is the title of a painting by a well-known South African artist, Brett Murray, exposing the genitals of the State president, Jacob Zuma. The painting was exhibited in a well-known Johannesburg establishment, the Goodman Gallery. In the last week of May 2012 the Johannesburg-based newspaper, *City Press*, published a photo of the painting. This led to a series of threats by the ANC, including a court case by Zuma in which he requested the High Court to rule on the protection of his dignity. The case was postponed (and later withdrawn) when a senior council for Zuma broke down emotionally when he spoke about the struggle against apartheid and the ongoing stereotyped portrayal of black people. The painting was sold to a German collector, but before it was removed from the gallery it was vandalized by two males acting independently of each other. The ANC branded the artist a racist, demanded that *City Press* and the gallery remove photos of the painting from their websites (to which they eventually agreed), requested a total boycott of *City Press*, and organized marches to the gallery. In a questionable move, an age restriction was placed on the painting by the Film Publications Board, an act outside of its jurisdiction. All this took place in a week of extreme public and media outcry. In parliament the ANC claimed that the painting and the political and racial emotion it stirred up has divided the country along racial lines and has awoken old racial tensions. Questions about the balance between the right to human dignity and freedom of expression were pushed to the fore. At the time of writing (June 2012) anger and shock were still being expressed by different parties, including the media, with the way the government had handled and politicized the matter, the whiff of censorship strongly redolent of the apartheid era, and the potential impact on future regulation and the protection of freedom of expression, including artistic expression. The leader of an opposition party, the Congress of the People (COPE), claimed that Zuma has violated his oath of office by failing to uphold his Constitutional obligation to protect the rights of the artist.

The above are only a few examples illustrating the tense relationship between the media and the government on freedom of expression and regulation of the media in general. Ongoing discourses about it often point out the fragility of the South African Democracy. The fact is that long after the end of apartheid, the freedom of the media as a pillar of Democracy is again under threat. Constantly threatening the media may, as under apartheid, lead to self-censorship. Self-censorship is a devastating mechanism which prevents the media from revealing potential atrocities committed by the government or any other social actor. In journalism education, the history of the media under apartheid and the effects of censorship are highlighted. The present situation is increasingly dealt with and paralleled to the past.

The discourses about freedom of expression also produce challenging discussions of what may be termed different cultural perceptions and understandings of key concepts such as "public interest" and "freedom of expression", with the government often claiming that the media still holds a Western-biased view and that there is a need to *indigenize* journalism and journalistic practices.

Theme Five: Indigenization and an African Media Ethic

A fifth theme, and closely related to the issue of freedom of expression and Democracy, is normative theory and questions related to the role and functions of journalism in society and journalism ethics. There is an increasing quest to address such theory and questions from an indigenous perspective.

In this respect the point of departure is that the role and functions of journalism and the journalist in society are mainly seen from a Western perspective and that Western-biased theory dominates journalism and media education. The argument is that the political economy of media systems in Africa is still guided and dominated by Western views and values related to ownership, control, management and journalism practices, and Western-dominated views of freedom of expression, public opinion and public interest. The questions to be asked and answered in journalism education are: How can media and journalism practices be indigenized, if at all? Should they even be indigenized? Will an indigenous theoretical framework contribute to more journalistic practices in line with African ethical tenets?

From this, and in line with some of the principles of the African moral philosophy of *ubuntuism*, there follows a view that the overall purpose of journalism is developmental, that it should stimulate community participation and be consensus-orientated, and therefore that it should be practiced in consultation with the community. In the context of the needs of developing countries, journalism should encourage action towards civic transformation and community renewal. In this process, journalism may need to ensure the well-being of the collective, rather than the protection of individual rights: it may be seen as a catalyst for *moral agency* and as such contribute to *moral literacy* (see e.g. Blankenberg 1999; Christians 2004; Louw 2004; Okigbo 1996; Shutte 2001).

Questions such as the following are raised: What is *ubuntuism*[8]? What kind of journalism might be born of an *ubuntu* framework? Can an *ubuntu* framework actually work for journalism practice and ethics?[9]

There is an ongoing debate as to the kind of journalism likely to emerge from an *ubuntuism* framework. Such a journalism might not place a high value on objectivity, neutrality and detachment, for instance—indeed, it might view objectivity as impossible or inopportune (Okigbo 1996). The journalist is seen to be an involved member of the community, one who cannot remain a spectator. Through the journalist's work, a voice must be given to the community. Active involvement and dialogue with the community rather than detachment in the name of objectivity and neutrality may be required from the journalist (Blankenberg 1999).

Regarding the requirement of factuality, the Western conception of truth is seen to hinge completely on facts, doing little to embed these facts in a network of cultural and social meanings generated within the community itself (Wasserman and De Beer 2004, 92). According to *ubuntuism*, values such as truth, freedom and justice cannot be dealt with independently from a community's (cultural and social) values.

In short, it appears that Western epistemological thinking about the functions of journalism in society proceeds from a focus on journalism primarily in terms of (1) its information, surveillance, entertainment and educational role, (2) journalism's freedom and right to protection in order to be able to fulfill its social responsibility, and (3) the individual's right to information, protection, entertainment and education. In *ubuntuism*, on the other hand, the emphasis is on journalism's role as an agent of community-bonding and dialogue towards reaching consensus based on the cultural and social values and morals of a community. The emphasis moves from the journalist as informant, gatekeeper, interpreter and educator to the journalist as mediator; from the journalist as observer to the journalist as participant and negotiator; from the journalist as a watchdog to the journalist as a guide-dog.

Obviously an *ubuntu* interpretation of journalism and the journalist's role and functions in society can have vast implications for the ways in which journalism may be practiced and, as far as ethics are concerned, it may turn upside-down the old Cartesian dualities which characterize journalism ethics (right/wrong, good/bad, emotion/reason, objective/subjective) (Keeble 2005, 56–64).

Given the impact an indigenous framework may have on the content and practices of journalism, it is an important theme in journalism education. It is mostly discussed in the contexts of the sociology, political economy and regulation of journalism. Most discussions revolve around the ethics of journalism and journalistic practices. The question is: What is an "African" journalistic perspective on matters related to privacy, public interest, public opinion, freedom of expression, objectivity, truth, etc., and how does it differ from what is seen to be almost universal practices?

With the above questions in mind, it was established in a recent study of the National Press Club that ethics is a central occupational need among journalists. The National Press Club Work Environment Survey (Consulta 2010), conducted among mainstream journalists and news reporters across the country, highlighted the lack of understanding and knowledge of ethics in journalists' working environments.

Despite the existence of codes of conduct, only 21 percent of respondents indicated that said code was referred to in the newsroom on a regular basis. The survey further revealed that only 55 percent of the respondents felt confident that editors had the authority to guarantee work environments that are conducive to ethical journalism. Forty-seven percent agreed that a culture to discuss ethical issues seemed to exist.

Issues such as lack of time, competition between newspapers, a focus on quantity rather than quality, rigorous deadlines, and the threats of increased censorship (see discussion of regulation and freedom of expression) were raised as some of the factors impacting on ethical standards.[10] The survey pointed out that action was needed to entrench the application of existing codes of ethics, and also that journalists needed more resources and more control over the use of copy.[11]

From the above, it is clear that indigenization can bring about a whole range of new journalistic skills and ethical practices.

Theme Six: The Impact of the New Media on Journalism

The new media and the challenges and issues it has created for journalism forms an integral if not defining part of contemporary journalism education. Besides the teaching of new (technical) journalism skills, the nature, use and consequences of the new media are also dealt with. Besides its technological and economic features, the new media defines to a great extent a new media and journalism culture.

The starting point is that an understanding of the characteristics of the new media and the media environment it has created should be the basis of journalists' knowledge of the new media. Such characteristics include:

- the new distribution platforms giving rise to multi-media and on-line approaches;
- an increased, huge diversity in choice between the various media and media platforms with the concepts of pluralism and diversity gaining new meaning(s) in the new media environment;
- the development of a high level of interactivity between communicators and users (audiences);
- the convergence of public and private media, such as the disappearance of the previously clear distinction between public, private (commercial) and community broadcasting systems;
- a blurring of media genres (as regards to content)—for instance "infotainment";
- changed audiences (tastes and uses) and niche markets with new tastes, uses, readership, viewing and on-line patterns (see e.g. Lowe and Hujanen 2003; Fourie 2010a, 2010b).

As far as the profession is concerned, journalism education is required to take note of the changes the new media have brought about, such as a more educated workforce, a stronger professional consciousness among journalists, new processes and techniques of production, and threats to the future of the print media (Heinonen and Luostarinen 2008; Reese 2008; Terzis 2009, 14). The environments in which journalists work across the various media platforms (print, radio, television, video, internet, mobile) are constantly evolving in response to new technological innovations, changing media policies, and changing audiences with changed and changing needs and expectations (see the National Press Club's study on work environment: Consulta 2010). All this affects journalists' employment, their perceptions of their professional roles, and their professional values and practices. As in the case of indigenization, the new media confronts education with a new range of skills to be mastered.

In a sense the changes to the profession have also created the so-called "crisis of journalism" (see e.g. Allan 2005, 1; Löffelholz, Weaver, and Schwarz 2008), which is also a focal point in South African journalism education.

The crisis relates to concerns about

- the commercialization of journalism and its influence on the quality of journalism;
- the rise of tabloid journalism;
- the impact of online journalism (and "do-it-yourself journalism", e.g. blogs, chat rooms, electronic interest groups, social media, etc.) on journalistic practices;
- journalism succumbing to technological determinism.

Questions are raised about the effect of the new media on key concepts such as "objectivity", "factuality", "engagement", "accountability", "public interest", "advocacy", "trust" and "authenticity". In this regard there is, like elsewhere in the world, concern that objectivity as a journalistic doctrine is in decay (especially on-line); that the mainstream media have become exceedingly opinionated; that although journalists seem to be committed to objectivity, they nevertheless see it as an unrealistic ideal; and, that objectivity does not guide journalists' decision-making.

Questions about these concepts become even more complex in South Africa when they are raised not only in terms of the nature of the new media, but also in the context of the above-discussed indigenous African framework.

Conclusion: Journalism Education and the Dichotomous South African Society

The discussion of the six themes above confirms that besides its focus on the teaching of (universal) journalism skills, South African journalism education is embedded in the socio-cultural and political realities of South African society. For this reason, journalism theory and discourses about journalism skills are to a large extent dominated by issues of race, gender, identity, development and democracy.

Characteristics of South African society (cf. Fourie 2010a) that specifically impact on South African journalism and journalism education are extreme diversities, dichotomies and paradoxes: rich versus poor, literate versus illiterate, urbanized versus rural, First World versus Third World conditions, developed versus under-developed, etc. This is a society that is characterized by a variety of cultures and languages and various racial and ethnic groups.[12] "New" racism and xenophobia, or a fear and distrust of "the other", linger on the periphery of the country's social dynamics. It is a crime- and fear-ridden society in which corruption is becoming the norm.[13] All these diversities affect education and need to be dealt with.

These social characteristics seep deeply into South African politics, day-to-day living, the economy, social structures and social behavior—and they all find expression in South African media and journalism. This affects media ownership, media regulation, the staffing of newsrooms, the content of journalism and how media users understand, experience and interpret journalism. It is within this society that the country's First World media system has to function and that journalism is practiced.[14]

The representation of this kind of society leads to a media and media content which is often criticized for its endemic focus on crime, corruption, violence, racial tension, poor governance, nepotism and corruption, and for the fact that it often does so in an alarmist, sensationalist and inflammatory way.

Part of the paradox of South African society is that it is also part of the First World and has not escaped the macro transformations characterizing the First World, such as the move towards Democracy. In terms of politics, the society has moved from apartheid to a multi-party democratic state with profound and far-reaching transformational consequences for all its institutions, ranging from a new Constitution to changed State, legal, economic, educational, military, social, health, cultural and media institutions.

Some of the outstanding consequences of democratization specifically affecting journalism and which journalism education constantly needs to take cognizance of are the emergence of a new kind of public characterized by hybridization, fragmentation and the growing power of labour unions and civil organizations. As elsewhere in the world, the changed South African society calls for a new conceptualization of the public sphere—one which is different from Habermas' ideal public sphere, that is one in which it is acknowledged that a single public sphere with a common normative dimension seldom exists and that it is difficult to recognize a coherent population with shared values.

In addition, and as in the rest of the developed world, South Africa is a society in which the traditional distinction between the public and the private is blurred. Given different kinds of social movements, new and different kinds of grassroots organizations and communities (real and virtual), public interest as such (i.e. what "public interest" is) has changed and is increasingly difficult to define. Against this background and with a rising pressure to indigenize and increasing questioning of "Western-biased" journalistic practices and skills, it is becoming more difficult for journalists to claim that they serve the public interest or to use the construct of "public interest" and/or "public opinion" in their defense.

Clearly, all of the above confront South African journalism education with new challenges.

NOTES

1. South Africa has 23 universities, a majority of which offer some programmes in journalism or journalism and media education and/or communication science. The main universities offering journalism and media education are: University of Fort Hare, University of Stellenbosch, University of Cape Town (film and media education), University of South Africa (Communication Science), Nelson Mandela Metropolitan University (Port Elizabeth), University of the Free State (Bloemfontein), Northwest University (Potchefstroom), University of the Witwatersrand (Johannesburg), University of Johannesburg, University of KwaZulu-Natal (Durban and Pietermaritzburg), University of Pretoria, University of Zululand (KwaDlangezwa). Formal tertiary education in journalism (and/or related media education, communication and cultural education) started in 1959 at the Potchefstroom University for Christian Higher Education (now renamed Northwest University). The program was informed by programs offered at that stage in the Netherlands, Belgium and Germany. Apart from universities, many former Technicons (now renamed Universities of Technology) offer journalism education. One of the most well-known is the Tshwane University of Technology (Pretoria). There are

also several private institutions offering diplomas and certificates in journalism. For in depth discussions of South African journalism education and training, see, e.g., Berger 2008; De Beer 2010; De Beer and Prince 2005; Garman 2005, McCurdy and Power 2007, Wasserman 2011.

2. Early representation theory can be found in Ancient Greek philosophy. Throughout the ages it has developed into several full-fledged theories in art, visual, perception and reception studies. Apart from the media *representing* the public, the most common understanding of representation in media and journalism education is the semiotic one, namely that representation is a socio-cultural and political schema for the interpretation and portrayal of a signifier (object/subject).

3. The Terzis (2009) study is a follow-up of the study by Stephenson and Mory (1990) which was commissioned by the European Commission and the European Journalism Training Association in response to the recognition by the European Commission of the powerful role and importance of the media.

4. South Africa has a population of 49.3 million and 11 official languages. The country has three public service television channels, one free-to-air television channel, one pay television (subscription) channel, and two satellite television pay services with over 160 channels. The country has six public service radio stations, 18 commercial national and regional radio stations, 10 public service African-language stations and over 60 community radio stations. As far as print is concerned, the country has 21 daily national, regional and city-based newspapers, 24 weekly newspapers and 25 community papers. There are over 400 consumer magazine titles and over 650 trade, technical and professional journals and annuals. There are 31 major cinema houses, each accommodating a number of screens. In terms of online media there are literally thousands of sites with 17 major media sites, not counting the online sites of newspapers, broadcasters, etc. (South Africa and SADC Media Facts 2011; OMD South Africa, http://www.omd.co.za, accessed June 6, 2012).

5. Chapter 2 of the South African Constitution is a Bill of Rights and deals with various human rights, including gender and sexual orientation. Clause 16 guarantees the freedom of the press and other media.

6. The Press Freedom Commission proposed significant reforms to South Africa's system of print media regulation aimed at strengthening its independence, enhancing its accessibility and deepening its credibility. Changes include: an increased role for representatives of the public in the processes and structures of the Press Council and a commensurately decreased role for press representatives. Effectively the system of "self-regulation" is replaced with independent co-regulation between the press and the public. Other recommendations include: the scrapping of the requirement that complainants waive their right of access to the courts; the broadening of the criteria for third-party complaints by people not directly affected; the imposition of "space fines"—which would compel newspapers to set aside determined amounts of space for apologies and reprimands; the imposition of monetary fines for consistent and serious non-compliance with the rulings of the ombudsman; the strengthening of "right of reply" requirements; increased protection for children; the physical separation of the office of the ombudsman from those of Print Media South Africa (PMSA) and Sanef (www.sanef.org.za, accessed May 30, 2012).

7. More than 30 non-governmental organizations, including academic associations, the Human Rights Commission, Corruption Watch, the Law Society of South Africa, the

Nelson Mandela Foundation, the Public Protector, Higher Education South Africa (HESA) and numerous media, non-governmental organizations such as the Right-to-Know (R2K) Campaign, the South African National Press Club and Sanef continuously protested against the Bill and presented new submissions to public hearings against the Bill. The government itself launched a pro-Bill advertising campaign which in its turn was severely criticized in the media and by opposition parties as being misleading, if not against the Constitution. The main objections are that the Bill offends the Constitutional values of openness, transparency and accountability and opposes freedom of expression; that it will prohibit the exposure of government incompetence, criminality, wrongdoing, abuse of authority and corruption, and that the absence of a public interest clause and the defense of public interest make the Bill unconstitutional. The main recommendations are that the Bill should only apply to intelligence matters.

8. The question "What is *ubuntuism*?" and its impact on journalism are addressed in more depth in Fourie (2007; also see Hamminga 2005; Nussbaum 2003). Here, suffice it to say that *ubuntuism* can be understood as a moral philosophy, a collective African consciousness deeply embedded in African culture's expression of communal (collective or shared) compassion, reciprocity, dignity, harmony and humanity in the interest of a community (traditionally the tribe or clan), with justice and mutual caring for all (see e.g. Nussbaum 2003, 1). An outstanding characteristic of *ubuntuism* is its emphasis on community and collectivity. *Ubuntuism* moves beyond an emphasis on the individual and individual rights, and places the emphasis on sharing and on individual participation in a collective life. Community is the context in which personhood is defined. As such, it differs from the emphasis on the self in mainstream Eurocentric moral philosophy. The essence of being is participation with other humans. Whereas Western individualistic Democracy insists on freedom of the self from intrusion by others, in *ubuntuism* a person's freedom depends for its exercise and fulfillment on personal relationships with others. A person is first and foremost a participatory being *dependent on others* for his/her development. *Ubuntuism* therefore places a high premium on negotiation, inclusiveness and tolerance.

9. Fourie (2007) raises five questions about *ubuntu* as a normative framework for journalism. He points out the vast consequences such a framework may have for journalism as the (ideally) objective representation of the world. The questions concern: (1) the relevancy of *ubuntuism* in the context of the changed nature of traditional African culture, (2) the claim that *ubuntuism* is *distinctively* an African moral philosophy, (3) moral philosophy's vulnerability to political exploitation, (4) *ubuntuism* as a normative theory in a globalized world and changed media environment, and (5) the serious implications an *ubuntu* approach may have for journalism practice (the "tricks of the trade" or professional practices as practiced universally in newsrooms).

10. It is issues such as these that Bourdieu (1993, 1998) refers to as the "*structural limitations*' of the profession. Minogue (2005) refers to these as the *corrupting devices* of journalism (Fourie 2012a).

11. The national independent research survey commissioned by the National Press Club highlights ethical challenges experienced by mainstream journalists (see http:www.nationalpressclub.co.za/research.html and http:www.nationalpressclub.co.za/releases/20110227.php).

12. As an example of underdevelopment, recent statistics in the United Nations Report on Development (2012) reveals that despite South Africa's lead as the richest country in

Africa, 40.7 percent of South African children die shortly after birth, 23.9 percent of the children under five are growth restrained, 56.6 percent will not reach the age of five, more than 23 percent of the South African population live in poverty and 17.4 percent earn less than 1 Euro a day. Life expectancy in South Africa is 53 (compared to 73 in Brazil), 9 million of South Africa's 18.6 million children live in poverty, one in three experience hunger, and one in five has lost one or both parents (*Beeld*, May 16, 2012).

13. There were 2.1 million serious crime cases registered in 2010/2011 in South Africa, of which 15,940 are for murder, 198,602 for assault with the purpose to inflict serious harm and 247,630 residential burglary cases (South African Police Service 2012).

14. See Note 4.

REFERENCES

Allan, Stuart, ed. 2005. *Journalism: Critical Issues*. Maidenhead, UK: Open University Press.

Ansu-Kyeremeh, Kwasi. [1997] 2005. "Communication, Education and Development: Exploring an African Cultural Setting." In *Indigenous Communication in Africa: Concept, Application and Prospects*, edited by Kwasi Ansu-Kyeremeh. Accra: Ghana University Press.

Banda, Fackson, Catherine Beukes-Amiss, Tanja Bosch, Winston Mano, Polly McLean, and Lynette Steenveld. 2007. "Contextualising Journalism Education and Training in Southern Africa." *Ecquid Novi: African Journalism Education* 28 (1–2): 156–175.

Berger, Guy. 1998. "Media and Democracy in Southern Africa." *Review of African Political Economy* 25 (1): 599–610.

Berger, Guy. 2007. "In Search of Journalism Education Excellence in Africa: Summary of 2006 UNESCO Project." *Ecquid Novi: African Journalism Education* 28 (1–2): 149–155.

Berger, Guy. 2008. "Towards Defining 'Potential Centres of Excellence' in African Journalism Training." *Journalism Practice* 2 (2): 147–162.

Blankenberg, Ngaira. 1999. "In Search of Real Freedom: *Ubuntu* and the Media." *Critical Arts* 13 (2): 42–65.

Bourdieu, Pierre. 1993. *The Field of Cultural Production: Essays on Art and Literature*. New York: Columbia University Press.

Bourdieu, Pierre. 1998. *On Television*. Translated by P. Ferguson. New York: New Press.

Christians, Clifford. 2004. "*Ubuntu* and Communitarianism in Media Ethics." *Ecquid Novi: African Journalism Education* 25 (2): 235–256.

Consulta. 2010. *National Press Club Work Environment Survey*. Pretoria: Consulta Research.

De Beer, Arnold, ed., 2000. "Focus on Media and Racism." *Ecquid Novi: African Journalism Education* 21 (2).

De Beer, Arnold. 2008. "South African Journalism Research. Challenging Paradigmatic Schism and Finding a Foothold in an Era of Globalization." In *Global Journalism Research. Theories, Methods, Findings, Future*, edited by Martin Löffelholz, David Weaver, and Andreas Schwarz 185–197. Malden, MA: Blackwell Publishing.

De Beer, Arnold. 2010. "Looking for Journalism Education Scholarship in Some Unusual Places: The Case of Africa." *Communicatio: South African Journal for Communication Theory and Research* 36 (2): 213–226.

De Beer, Arnold, and Eitan Prince. 2005. "Editorial: Journalism Education Findings Its Way into the 2000s." *Ecquid Novi: African Journalism Education* 26 (2): 139–141.

Downing, John, and Charles Husband. 2005. *Representing "Race". Racisms, Ethnicities and the Media*. London: Sage.

Fourie, Pieter J. 2002. "Rethinking the Role of the Media in South Africa." *Communicare* 21 (1): 17–41.

Fourie, Pieter J. 2005. "Journalism Studies: Thinking about Journalists' Thinking." *Ecquid Novi: African Journalism Education* 26 (2): 142–159.

Fourie, Pieter J. 2007. "Moral Philosophy As the Foundation of Normative Media Theory: The Case of African Ubuntuism." *Communications* 32: 1–29.

Fourie, Pieter J. 2009. "'n Terugkeer na die onderdrukking van vryheid van spraak? Ooreenkomste tussen die apartheidsregering(s) en die ANC se optrede teen die media [A Return to the Repression of Freedom of Speech? Similarities between the Apartheid Government(s) and the ANC's Actions against the Media]." *Tydskrif vir Geesteswetenskappe* 49 (1): 62–84.

Fourie, Pieter J.. 2010a. "'New' Paradigms, 'New' Theory and Four Priorities for South African Mass Communication and Media Research." *Critical Arts* 24 (2): 173–192.

Fourie, Pieter J. 2010b. "The Past, the Present and the Future of South African Journalism Research [In Search of a Meta-theory for South African Journalism Research]." *Communicatio: South African Journal for Communication Theory and Research* 36 (2): 148–172.

Fourie, Pieter J. 2011. "Thinking about Journalists' Thinking (Two)." *Journal of African Media Studies* 3 (3): 309–327.

Fourie, Pieter J. 2012a. "Fundamentele massakommunikasienavorsing as 'n voorwaarde vir gesubstansieerde mediakritiek [Fundamental Mass Communication Research As a Precondition for Substantiated Media Criticism]." *Tydskrif vir Geestesetenskappe* 52 (1): 85–103.

Fourie, Pieter J. 2012b. "Revisiting communications policy in South Africa and the Global South." In *Ringtones of Opportunity: Policy, technology and access in Caribbean communications*, edited by Hopeton Dunn, 40–61. Kingston: Ian Randle Publications.

Garman, Anthea. 2005. "Teaching Journalism to Produce 'Interpretative Communities' Rather Than Just 'Professionals'." *Ecquid Novi: African Journalism Education* 26 (2): 199–211.

Hamminga, Bert. 2005. "Epistemology from the African Point of View." Accessed April 15. http://mindphiles.com/floor/philes/epistemo/epistemo.htm.

Heinonen, Ari, and Heikki Luostarinen. 2008. "Reconsidering 'Journalism' for Journalism Research." In *Global Journalism Research. Theories, Methods, Findings, Future*, edited by Martin Löffelholz, David Weaver and Andreas Schwarz, 227–240. Malden, MA: Blackwell Publishing.

Keeble, Richard. 2005. "Journalism Ethics: Towards an Orwellian Critique?" In *Critical Issues*, edited by Stuart Allan, 54–67. Maidenhead, UK: Open University Press.

Löffelholz, Martin, David Weaver, and Andreas Schwarz, eds., 2008. *Global Journalism Research. Theories, Methods, Findings, Future*. Malden, MA: Blackwell Publishing.

Louw, Dirk. 2004 "*Ubuntu*: An African Assessment of the Religious Other." http://www.by.edy/wcp/Papers/Afri/AfriLouw.htm.

Lowe, Gregory, and Taisto Hujanen, eds., 2003. *Broadcasting and Convergence: New Articulations of the Public Service Remit*. Göteborg: Nordicom.

Makhanya, Mondli. 2009. "Tackling Our Racial Fault Lines Is Much More Urgent than Apologies." *Sunday Times*, November 22.

McCurdy, Patrick M., and Gerry Power. 2007. "Journalism Education As a Vehicle for Media Development in Africa: The AMDI Project." *Ecquid Novi: African Journalism Education* 28 (1–2): 127–147.

Milo, Dario. 2010. "Chilly Winds Are Blowing around South African Media." *Mail and Guardian*, January 29.

Minogue, Kenneth. 2005. "Journalism: Power without Responsibility". *The New Criterion* 23 (6). http://newcriterion.com/archives/23/02/journalism-power-without-responsibility/.

Morrison, Joy. 2005. *Forum Theatre: A Cultural Forum of Communication, Kwasi Ansu-Kyeremeh, Kwasi 1997/2005 Communication, Education and Development: Exploring an African Cultural Setting*. Accra: Ghana University Press.

Nussbaum, Barbara. 2003. "African Culture and *Ubuntu*. Reflections of a South African in America. World Business Academy." *Perspectives* 17 (1): 1–12.

Okigbo, Charles. 1996. "Contextualising Freire in African Sustainable Development." *Africa Media Review* 10 (1): 31–54.

Prinsloo, Jeanne. 2010. "Journalism Education in South Africa: Shifts and Dilemmas." *Communicatio: South African Journal for Communication Theory and Research* 36 (20): 185–199.

Reese, Stephen, D. 2008. "Theorizing a Globalized Journalism." In *Global Journalism Research. Theories, Methods, Findings, Future*, edited by Martin Löffelholz, David Weaver and Andreas Schwarz, 240–253. Malden, MA: Blackwell Publishing.

Reid, Julie. 2012. "Press Freedom Commission, ANC and the Little Guy." *Daily Maverick*. http://www.1.dailymaverick.co.za/article/2012-05-02-press-freedom-commission-anc-.

Sanef (South African National Editors' Forum). 2003. *The Glass Ceiling and Beyond (I). The Status of Women and Diversity in the South African News Media*. Johannesburg: Sanef.

Sanef (South African National Editors' Forum). 2007. *The Glass Ceiling and Beyond (II). An audit of Women and men in South African Newsrooms*. Johannesburg: Sanef. http://www.sanef.org.za/resources/piblications.

Shutte, Augustine. 2001. *Ubuntu: An Ethic for a New South Africa*. Pietermaritzburg: Cluster Publications.

South African Human Rights Commission (SAHRC). 2000. *Faultlines: Inquiry into Racism in the Media*. Johannesburg: South African Human Rights Commission.

South African Police Service. 2012. "Crime Statistics Report. 2010/2011." http://www.Info.gov.za/view/DownloadFileAction?id=150105.

South Africa and SADC Media Facts, and Koenderman, T. 2011. *AdReview* in association with Finweek. Auckland Park, Johannesburg. http://www.omd.co.za/media_facts/samedia-facts2011.pdf.

Sparks, Colin. 2009. "South African Media in Transition." *Journal of African Media Education* 1 (2): 1–29.

Steenveld, Lynette. 2007. "The SAHRC's Enquiry into Racism and the Media: Problematising State–Media Relationships." *Ecquid Novi: African Journalism Education* 28 (1–2): 106–126.

Steenveld, Lynette. 2008. "Media and Race." In *Policy, Management and Media Representation. Vol. 2 of Media Studies*. 2nd ed., edited by Pieter J. Fourie, 277–302. Cape Town: Juta.

Stephenson, H., and P. Mory. 1990. *Journalism Training in Europe*. Brussels: Commission of the European Communities.

Steyn, Elanie, and Arnold De Beer. 2002. *Sanef's "2002 South African National Journalism Skills Audit", Final Report*. http://www.sanef.org.za.

Steyn, Elanie, Arnold De Beer, and Derik Steyn. 2005. *Sanef Skills Audit Phase 2: Managerial Competencies among First-line News Managers in South Africa's Mainstream Media Newsrooms, Final Report*. http://www.sanef.org.za.

Teer-Tomaselli, Ruth, and Keyan Tomaselli. 2001. "Transformation, Nation-building and the South African Media, 1993–1999." In *Media, Democracy and Renewal in Southern Africa*, edited by Keyan Tomaselli and H. Dunn, 123–180. Colorado Springs, CO: International Academic Publishers.

Terzis, Giorgios, ed. 2009. *European Journalism Education*. Bristol, UK: Intellect.

Tomaselli, Keyan. 2000. "Faulting 'Faultlines': Racism in the South African Media." *Ecquid Novi: African Journalism Education* 21 (2): 157–174.

Tomaselli, Keyan. 2009. "(Afri)Ethics, Communitarianism and Libertarianism." *The International Communication Gazette* 71 (7): 1–18.

Tomaselli, Keyan, and Mark Caldwell. 2002. "Journalism Education: Bridging Media and Cultural Education." *Communicatio: South African Journal for Communication Theory and Research* 28 (1): 22–28.

Wasserman, Herman. 2005a. "Debating the Media, Shaping Identity: Postcolonial Discourse and Public Criticism." *Communicatio: South African Journal for Communication Theory and Research* 31 (1): 49–61.

Wasserman, Herman. 2005b. "Journalism Education As Transformative Praxis." *Ecquid Novi: African Journalism Education* 26 (2): 159–174.

Wasserman, Herman. 2006a. "Globalized Values and Postcolonial Responses: South African Perspectives on Normative Media Ethics." *The International Communication Gazette* 68 (1): 71–91.

Wasserman, Herman. 2006b. "Redefining Media Ethics in the Post-colonial Context: Contending Frameworks in the South African Media." In *Media in South Africa after Apartheid: A Cross Media Assessment*, edited by A. Olorunnisola, 255–276. Lewiston, NY: The Edwin Mellen Press.

Wasserman, Herman. 2011. "Global Journalism Education: Beyond Panoramas." *Communicatio: South African Journal for Communication Theory and Research* 37 (1): 100–117.

Wasserman, Herman, and Arnold De Beer. 2004. "Covering HIV/AIDS. Towards a Heuristic Comparison between Communitarian and Utilitarian Ethics." *Communicatio: South African Journal for Communication Theory and Research* 30 (2): 84–98.

White, Robert. 2008. "Grassroots Participatory Communication: Is a New Vision of Communication Emerging in Africa." *African Communication Research* 1 (1): 11–45.

Index

Note:
Page numbers in **bold** type refer to figures
Page numbers in *italic* type refer to tables
Page numbers followed by 'n' refer to notes